YOU ARE FREAKING AMAZING

4 MOTIVATIONAL BOOKS IN 1 (SELF CARE, SMALL TALK, MINIMALISM & SELF TALK)

ASTON SANDERSON

WALNUT PUBLISHING

CONTENTS

PART IV
MINIMALIST LIVING

FOREWORD

Dear Reader,

I am so excited to bring you my first book collection, "You Are Freaking Amazing." The four books included within are very special to me, and I hope they will be special to you.

All four books — "Small Talk", "Self Care," "Minimalism" & "Self Talk"— come from a very personal place for me, and I wrote them as much for my readers as for myself. There's a saying that the advice you give other people is the advice you most need to hear, and I think that is true for me with a lot of the motivational material that I write. For example, I wrote "Self Talk" during a time I was feeling unconfident and stressed about where my career was going. I noticed that I was often my own worst critic, and I had negative thoughts swirling in my head.

I have studied psychology at the collegiate level, and though I hold no official degrees or licenses in the mental health field, it is a passion of mine to study. As the ideas of the books formed for me, I went deep into research for the books and for my own sanity, to help me turn what I felt were my greatest flaws into my greatest allies.

The result is the book you have in your hands now. Across all these different topics, you will learn not only how to become more amazing, but how to find the strength within yourself to realize how amazing *you already are*.

Over the years, I have received numerous emails and message from readers who have said these books have changed their lives, and have become resources they return to again and again. My hope is that the same will be true for you with my books, collected here for the first time.

Spreading these positive messages — that we can be kind to ourselves in our thoughts in "Self Talk," that we can free ourselves from our things in "Minimalist Living," that we can communicate with others in authentic and deep ways in "Small Talk," that we can love ourselves as much as we love others in "Self Care" — is why I write, and I hope you will find the ideas as impactful as I have.

Thank you for reading, and remember: You are freaking amazing.

Aston Sanderson

PART I

SELF TALK

HOW TO TRAIN YOUR BRAIN TO TURN NEGATIVE THINKING INTO POSITIVE THINKING & PRACTICE SELF LOVE

SELF TALK

HOW TO TRAIN YOUR BRAIN TO TURN NEGATIVE THINKING INTO POSITIVE THINKING & PRACTICE SELF LOVE

ASTON SANDERSON

INTRODUCTION

Do you sometimes feel like your thoughts are racing, or you are your own worst critic? These feelings are quite common. Even if you don't feel this way, though, chances are: You talk to yourself. We all do.

Talking to yourself is what we refer to as "self talk." It is the ingrained patterns of thoughts that we run through our head, often unconsciously, day in and day out. It is the way we talk to ourselves *about* ourselves. For most of us, it's a habit we've probably never consciously thought about before.

In this book, we'll cover everything you need to know about self talk to use it to your advantage, instead of letting it control you unconsciously. Self talk has incredible impact on your self confidence, your progress toward your goals, your relationships, and even the way you live your life.

After you read this book, you'll have concrete strategies (and exercises at the end of each chapter) to make your self talk your own greatest ally in living your best life possible.

This quick-read will help you turn negative self talk into constructive, positive self talk.

I sincerely hope you enjoy reading this book and that you find it helpful to you.

As an author, reviews help my book reach more people. If you like this book or find it helpful in any way, I ask that you please leave me a review. I personally read all my reviews and love to hear from readers.

If you find any errors in this book or have suggestions for improvements, I would love to hear them. You can reach me at aston@walnutpub.com.

Sincerely,

Aston

WHAT IS SELF TALK?

In this chapter, we'll discuss just what exactly "self talk" refers to, so we're all on the same page as we move forward in this book.

Self talk is your internal monologue. It is the thoughts that go through your head on a daily basis. Usually, it is how you talk to yourself about yourself. You may have never thought about your self talk before, or you may be aware of it. Either way, you'll learn a lot more in this book about harnessing your self talk for your own benefit.

The thing about self talk is that we all have it. While writing this book, I can't even count how many times I've talked to myself about it. I've said things like, "I didn't get enough writing done today," or "I should have started working earlier today." I'm sure you have a lot of similar thoughts when you are trying to complete a large project. Together, we'll learn how to better deal with these thoughts.

Our first step is to better understand self talk, so let's look at what it is.

Self Talk is Often Judgmental

Is your self talk mainly negative, or mainly positive? There's also the option of neutral thoughts. You have probably heard of "negative self talk" and "positive self talk," but maybe not "neutral self talk."

LET'S look at examples of all three:

Positive self talk:

- I am a good person
- My body is beautiful
- I killed it during my work presentation today

Negative self talk:

- I am not good enough
- I really need to lose 5 pounds
- I won't do well during my presentation tomorrow

Neutral self talk:

- I am a human
- I weigh 150 pounds
- I have spent 2 hours preparing for my presentation tomorrow

The neutral self talk examples probably feel a bit strange. They are simply facts, and two of them are quantifiable, meaning they are able to be measured by numbers.

When we talk to ourselves, we most often use judgmental self talk, whether we are judging ourselves positively or negatively. Our brain already knows facts, it doesn't need to state them "aloud" to itself. Our brain is meant for *processing* those facts. When we talk to ourselves, we are usually working through how we feel about something, whether that is our weight, our performance at work, or our general sense of self-worth.

Can you think of any things you've said to yourself about yourself recently?

In the next section, we'll look at how self talk shapes our lives.

Self Talk is the Story We Tell Ourselves

AS A PROFESSIONAL STORYTELLER, I am especially invested in the power narratives hold over humans.

Storytelling is one of the most basic human needs, I believe. It is how we communicate with each other, how we pass down important culture, impart life lessons, and understand the world and our lives that are most often full of chaos, coincidence, and unpredictability.

We are all the main characters of our own stories. You are the leading woman (or man) of your life story. No matter the position you find yourself in today, you are probably creating stories to shape the past, your ideas about the future, and even your present self.

For example, maybe you tell yourself a story about graduating from a college with a bad reputation, so that is why you struggled to find your first job. Or maybe your story is that the college with a bad reputation forced you to work harder to prove your skills, so it was an asset to you, instead of a hindrance. Either way, the fact is the same about where you graduated from. It's just the story you shape around it to explain what it means to you and your life.

Maybe you have a story in your head about the future, like the best-selling mystery novel you will write. Maybe your story is daydreaming about going to the movie premiere from your book adaptation, and how glamorous it will be. Maybe your story is your friends and family laughing at you when they read your novel, thinking it is a piece of drivel. None of these things have happened, but they are all stories and judgments you are making up about the future, and they affect you right now, and the approach you take to writing that book (or putting it off forever).

In the present, self talk can feel kind of like a sports announcer, narrating our every move. In a soccer match or baseball game, however, the players can't hear the running commentary on their actions, so it doesn't affect them. But what if the players could *hear* the sportscaster saying, *"Ouch, what a bad pass that was,"* or *"He takes the plate with a low batting average this season. The odds are against him that he'll get this hit."* It would certainly change their performance! That's often how our own self talk can be — a constant (and not very friendly) announcement of our previous errors in a similar situation, recent mistakes we've made, how the odds are against us succeeding, and that our general stats are not good. To attempt to perform without hearing this constant chatter would be like being on the baseball diamond and needing to tune out a loudspeaker broadcasting your actions to thousands. Even though we're the only ones that can hear our self talk, tuning it out is not very easy.

No matter whether you are thinking about the past, future or present, you are creating stories by talking to yourself. These stories are not harmless; in fact, they shape your whole worldview and approach to life. The more you tell yourself the same stories over and over, the more true they become to you, whether they have basis in reality or not. And you may be entirely unaware of them! That's why in this book, I want to give you the tools to become aware of your self talk, and use it to help you shape the narrative about you and your life. With healthy self talk, you can reframe past events, understand yourself better in the present, and take action toward achieving what you want in the future. Harnessing your self talk can be supremely powerful, as you'll see.

Now that you better understand how self talk is the story we tell ourselves, before we get down to the nitty gritty of investigating and reshaping your own self talk, let's look at 7 types of negative self talk.

Types of Negative Self Talk

As we go through this book, we will learn to identify our negative self talk, how to investigate it, how to use more positive self talk in our lives, and other strategies for using our inner chatter to our advantage, to lead happier lives and achieve our goals. Our first task will be identifying negative self talk, so let's define 7 different kinds of *negative* self talk.

Filtering

Filtering can affect other types of self talk, and it is probably the most common form. The idea behind filtering is that when 10 good things happen to us, and one bad thing, we only remember the one bad thing. For example, if you received 10 compliments on a painting you created, but one insult, you'd probably only remember the insult, and you'd think about it a lot more, even though you got 10 times more compliments. Our brains are actually more inclined to remember negatives rather than positives due to evolution. It was helpful in caveman times, when you really needed to remember that a certain watering hole is where you almost got attacked by a lion, as it could save your life. Today, though, remembering and going over and over in our head the insults lobbed at us does little to help us lead better lives.

EXAMPLE OF FILTERING: "Even though everyone said they loved my haircut, Jen said it was 'interesting.' Everyone else must be wrong, and only Jen is telling me the truth that my new haircut looks bad."

CATASTROPHIZING

Do you ever find yourself going down a "thought spiral?" When one bad thing happens, does it suddenly remind you of all the things you are unhappy with in your life? This is catastrophizing. When one thing goes wrong, it seems everything goes wrong, or that one thing is blown way out of proportion.

EXAMPLE OF CATASTROPHIZING: "I was late to work this morning. I probably looked disheveled when I walked in. Everyone probably thinks I'm a screw-up. I probably won't get that promotion now. And I have to go to the happy hour after work, and I'm always bad at socializing. And if it goes late, I'll be tired again tonight. I don't perform well when I'm tired, just like that huge history exam in high school that I bombed. I'll probably oversleep again tomorrow. I can't do anything right."

PERSONALIZING

There is one main difference between optimists and pessimists. Optimists distance themselves from thinking about the negative things in life as a personal attack on them, and easily embrace what is positive in life. Pessimists tend to make excuses for reasons why the positive things that happen are flukes, and embrace worst-case scenarios as the norm and what they attract from the universe. Personalizing is making external events a reflection of you, even if they actually aren't. So when bad things happen, a pessimist, or someone who is using this tactic of negative thinking, will find a reason that they are to blame or caused it. It can be known as *internalizing,* and it also means taking external events a little too personally.

EXAMPLE OF PERSONALIZING: "Jim said the party seemed 'quiet,' he probably meant that no one fun was there, even though I was. He thinks I'm not fun to hang out with."

POLARIZING

In polarization, events or traits are seen as either 100% good or 100% bad. There is no in-between or gray area. Often, this kind of self talk goes hand-in-hand with perfectionism. If something isn't totally perfect, you may see it as a total waste. This kind of thinking is dangerous because even for largely negative events, there is often a silver lining. Even from largely positive events, there are still sometimes lessons to be learned for the future. Seeing the good and bad in most things is a more productive way to approach life and self talk.

EXAMPLE OF POLARIZING: "I had one of my slowest runs this week, so my whole week of workouts was a wash. Why can't I get better and faster?"

REHASHING

Rehashing can also be known as *ruminating* or *dwelling*. Rehashing means thinking about the past, but in a negative, unproductive, and circular manner. Your thoughts may go over and over past events, leading you to wonder how things could have turned out differently if you had just won the game, not said the stupid thing, not gone to the party, not woken up late, not invested in that business, tried harder in school, etc., etc. and on and on. Often, rehashing can be associated with feelings of guilt or shame about things that have happened in the past that affect our self-esteem today.

EXAMPLE OF REHASHING: "If I just hadn't stayed late at the office that one night, my wife would have changed her mind about the divorce."

REHEARSING

Rehearsing is the opposite side of the coin of rehashing. Rehearsing is thinking about the future, but in a circular and unproductive fashion as well. This type of self talk often happens when we are nervous about an event in the future, or feel the future is too uncertain. We may be going over and over imagined conversations in our head, the different reactions we will get from people to our work we deliver, or imagining each step of our date. Preparing for the future has its place, for sure. But it becomes unhealthy when we become preoccupied with thinking about the future instead of focusing on the present, which is when we take action to prepare for the future.

EXAMPLE OF REHEARSING: "When everyone challenges my idea during the meeting, I'll make sure to bring up the failed team project from last year. I'll say..."

BLAMING

The last of the 7 types of self talk is blaming. Blaming can easily fall into a negative self talk pattern that is hard to escape from. Blaming happens when we feel responsible for someone else's feelings of pain, or our own pain.

EXAMPLE OF BLAMING: "Olivia wasn't having a good day, and I wasn't able to make her laugh. I'm a terrible friend."

NOW THAT YOU know a lot more about what self talk is, we'll look at why negative self talk is so harmful in the next chapter.

Exercise: Which Type of Self Talk Do You Recognize?

THE EXERCISE for this chapter is to choose which of the 7 types of negative self talk you identify with most. Is there one type that you know you use to talk yourself daily? Or most recently? This exercise will get you started in connecting your own self talk to what you read in this book.

.

WHY IS NEGATIVE SELF TALK BAD?

Negative self talk can be hugely detrimental to us. It holds us back from achieving what we want, it keeps us feeling low, and it can just generally feel pretty crappy to have those thoughts racing through you head all the time. But there's good news, too. Turning your negative self talk around into positive self talk can mean that you have the self-confidence to achieve what you want, feel good about yourself, and feel happier without all those negative thoughts in your head.

In this chapter, we'll discuss in more detail the ways that self talk is harmful to us.

Your Own Worst Critic

Self talk generally makes you feel down on yourself. Often-times, we are our own worst critics. Our friends and family would never be as cruel to us as we are to ourselves in our own head. Like it was mentioned in the last chapter, our brains are wired to focus on the negative. So when it comes to ourselves, we can feel there's a lot that we don't like.

Maybe you feel down on your body or your weight, maybe you feel down on your skills or work performance, maybe you feel bad about your current or past relationships. The list can go on and on! Certainly, (and hopefully) we all have areas in which we have positive self talk as well. The importance is knowing in which areas we can be more susceptible to self criticism.

Saps Your Energy

Do you ever feel like your thoughts are racing when you feel something has not gone right, or you are feeling down on yourself? Often, having negative self talk in our head can be pretty draining for our mental energy. It takes a lot of effort to continually criticize ourselves day in and day out. Even if your negative self talk feels automatic and unconscious, it is still taking energy out of you.

That leaves less energy for making good decisions, assessing problems or situations accurately instead of skewed toward the negative, and using our brains for creative thinking, problem solving, work, or enjoying the moment. Feeling excessively worried or drained mentally is not something anyone enjoys.

Venting to Yourself

Sometimes people say that venting our frustrations can make them have less power of us, and venting is a healthy outlet for anger or annoyance. But for many people, venting only makes matters worse. Being annoyed by something is the first step, but then complaining about it is the second step to really cementing it in your brain. Venting can be helpful in some cases, but not many, especially not for small annoyances that we'd forget and move on if it weren't for talking about them all the time.

Can you think of that one super-negative relative you have? We all have someone in our lives like Uncle Steven who just won't stop complaining about "how awful the potato salad was at Aunt Mary's church barbecue last weekend, and how there were too many flies, why didn't she put out more fly traps? And auto repair shop Danny was there, and isn't he annoying, how many stories did he tell about his Yorkshire terrier digging up the garden, again?"

These may have been minor annoyances to Uncle Steve at the time, but now that he's been raving to anyone who will listen for weeks, they are causing him more distress now, even though the events are long in the past. He's making himself miserable, and some people seem to just love being miserable.

(Apologies to all actual Uncle Stevens who may be reading, by the way, I'm sure you're lovely people. If you're not, well, keep reading this book!)

Negative, internal self talk can follow the same pattern as venting out loud: It's almost as if you are venting about things, but to yourself. If something annoys you, and you say that to yourself in your head, it's effectively Uncle Steven sharing his story with everyone around him. Sure, you're not going on and on, but it's still creating a narrative in your head. When you go around and around in circular patterns, these things become routine, more memorable, and easily accessible.

Should You Trust Your Brain?

There is one last way that negative self talk can make you unhappy: If left unregulated, it can run wild, become routine, and get "stuck" in the same old patterns. Just like all humans get a bit "stuck" in our habits and ways of doing things, our thought patterns can get stuck, too.

Sometimes, we identify too closely with our thoughts. Remember that you are not your thoughts, and we will discuss this more in-depth in another chapter. If we trust that everything our brain tells us is true, we just believe any thought we can come up with. And as humans are extremely creative, we can come up with a lot of ways to negatively talk to ourselves and criticize ourselves.

But you shouldn't trust your brain, especially when it comes to negative self talk patterns you've been experiencing for years. Your brain may just be stuck. It takes more brain power, at first, to break these harmful patterns. But once you establish new patterns, the positive self talk patterns will be easier to maintain. Your brain is especially prone to tricking you when you are feeling emotionally bad. When you're in a bad mood, it's almost like you are wearing negative self talk glasses. Everything can seem to be going wrong. For example, if you're feeling in a low mood and it starts raining, you may groan and think about how rain is so depressing, how you forgot your umbrella, and how the rest of the day is ruined. However, if you're in a good mood, it's easier to see things through a positive lens. If it rains, you may feel happy thinking about all the flowers that will now bloom, or appreciate how the sound of rainfall is extremely peaceful.

Noticing our negative self talk when it's happening, and noticing our emotional state, will be helpful to changing those patterns as we go through this process together.

In the next chapter, we will address the myriad benefits to be gained by changing your self talk patterns.

Exercise: Your Inner Critic's Favorite Topic

The exercise for this chapter is to determine what area of your life your inner critic loves to chat about most through negative self talk. Is it your work? A specific past event? A relationship? Your body? Try to figure out which area your inner critic tackles the most with self talk, so you can move forward reading this book with an idea of what area you'd like to silence your inner critic in. Do not feel pressure to nail it down now, however. You can keep reading and learn more first.

BENEFITS OF CHANGING SELF TALK

I n this chapter, we'll briefly discuss a few ways that changing your self talk from a negative state to more positive patterns will help you in your life. There really are so many benefits you'll see in every area of your life. It can help you feel happier, sleep more soundly, worry less, improve your relationships, improve your work, and help you in any area you feel you are struggling.

More Resilient

Resiliency is the ability to adapt to change and recover or work through bad experiences or setbacks. By learning more about the unconscious language your brain is constantly running, and gaining more control over it, you will better understand your reactions to things, your habits and yourself. When you are able to gain that distance from your own thought patterns, you are able to more accurately judge external circumstances. For example, if you aren't aware of your negative self talk, and your loan for a home gets denied, you may spiral into worry, stress, and low self-esteem, blaming yourself for the situation. However, if you are aware of your self talk and notice you are starting to blame yourself and throw a pity party, you can take a step back, recognize your reaction, and turn it into more positive self talk. You can recognize that this situation is not ideal, but think to yourself that you are resourceful, you have a big network, and you can figure out what steps you need to take to re-apply for the loan and get it approved and make a plan.

When you have more positive self talk, you don't get stuck in the trap of reacting to external events very emotionally. Your mental state will be stronger when bad times come, as they are sure to do at some point in all of our lives.

More Time for Creativity and Enjoyment

When you let go of a lot of negative self talk, you free up a lot of mental energy that you can put towards your work, being more creative, and enjoying the present moment instead of worrying about the future or rehashing the past. As mentioned in the last chapter, the inner chatter of our self criticism can take up a lot of space in our brain and use up a lot of our brain power. When you can stop those harmful patterns and circular thinking, you will have more time for creative thinking, or just relaxed, restful enjoyment of the moment.

Become a Better Leader

Negative self talk can lead to negative self esteem. When we feel badly about ourselves, it comes across in our body language, our actions, and our conversations. Have you ever heard the phrase, "confidence is sexy?" When people are confident, you can just tell. When they are nervous, it is also easy to see.

If you have more positive self talk going on in your mind, your actions, the way you carry yourself, the way you talk, it will all start to follow this more positive thought pattern you have running in the back of your mind. If you are in any kind of leadership position, it will make you a better leader, as people want to follow someone who is confident.

Self doubt affects your actions, and if you don't appear confident, others will question you more, too. This is especially important in leadership roles, but really, in any area of life, no matter your position. With enough work with your self talk, you will inspire yourself more, and eventually, others.

Achieve Your Goals

You may find that retraining your thought patterns also affects your behavior. As your self talk becomes more positive, your actions will become more positive, too. That's the idea behind the psychology of Cognitive Behavioral Therapy, which believes that thoughts influence feelings, and feelings influence actions. That's a very broad topic for another time, so for now we'll leave it at an example:

Talking negatively to yourself might lead to feeling badly about yourself, and then eating a whole pan of brownies to make yourself feel better emotionally, which then leads to beating yourself up about the brownies, etc. etc. But if you stop the negative thoughts before eating the brownies, and just think, "I feel down about myself right now, but this is just a low point, and I know I will feel better later," instead of thought spiraling, you can clearly *see* your thought pattern. Thinking "I am enough," even if you don't feel perfect all the time, can be enough to stop harmful actions that will make you feel even worse.

Did you know that athletes use purposeful and intentional self talk as a training strategy? When athletes don't harness self talk in their mind properly, their thoughts can naturally bend toward the negative and the critical. Many coaches have a mental training regimen for their athletes as well as a physical one, and it includes how athletes talk to themselves during training, before a big race or match, during their athletic event, and after. Positive and realistic self talk can be used to win Olympic medals, as it puts athletes in the right frame of mind to achieve what they want, and perform to the best of their ability when it matters most.

It is the same way in our own lives, for anything we want to achieve. Want to get a promotion at work? Want to write a novel? Want to start a business? No matter what your goals are, you can look at achieving them the same way that athletes do their goals. By using self talk as a motivational tool, you can become more productive and achieve what you actually want to in life. Achieving the goals we feel most passionate about is one of the hardest things to do. And making our dreams come true begins with our inner mental chatter.

Inner Peace

Sometimes, the insides of our minds feel like a battlefield. Our thoughts are like shots fired in a war between our rational selves, our optimistic selves, and our negative selves. Having all that back and forth is tiring, unproductive and stressful.

When you have more positive self talk, or are able to just gain distance from your negative self talk, you can feel more at peace with yourself. Your brain may be quieter or at least more friendly in its incessant chatter. When you recognize all these different thoughts and where they come from, you can pacify the different warring sides of yourself. Achieve more feelings of inner peace by going through the methods in this book.

Changing External Circumstances

Before we move on to the next chapter, there is one more important thing to note about the benefits of self talk. Often, we think we need to improve our lives by changing our external circumstances. We just need a new job, to lost 5 pounds, to find a boyfriend or girlfriend, or to buy a material object like the newest iPhone or gadget.

But changing your exterior circumstances will not change your tendency toward the negative when you have negative self talk patterns ingrained in your brain.

You may have negative thoughts about your body like "I am so fat. I don't like the way I look."

In our heads, we imagine that when we get skinny, we will magically have positive thought patterns. We imagine we will start looking in the mirror and saying, "Wow, I am so skinny and beautiful!" But even if you change your body, your negative thought patterns will remain the same. Once you have lost the 10 pounds you aim to lose, then you will look in the mirror and see new flaws to criticize, as that is the way your brain has been used to thinking. You may think, "I could lose more fat on my stomach," or "Why can't I build muscle in my arms? They still look flabby." Or, "I have no butt." And on and on. A pattern of negative thinking will stay a pattern. Our minds our quite creative; we can always find something to criticize. We will find more and more things for our negative mind to spin around in endless circles, and there will always be one more thing we need to change, no matter what.

However, if you change your ways of thinking, then you can set realistic goals, achieve them, and feel happy with your results. So, maybe health is something you'd like to change. You can still feel that you want to change your weight, as long as you know your brain will not magically change from unhappy to happy once you achieve it. In fact, with more positive and realistic thought patterns, instead of excessively negative ones, you will probably have an easier time achieving your goals of weight loss than with self-hating, self-defeating thoughts.

Are you ready to start moving forward with retraining your inner chatter? In the next chapter, we'll delve into how we will go about changing your self talk.

Exercise: See the Difference Between Your Negative Self Talk and Imagined Positive Self Talk

THINK of a goal you have that you have negative thoughts around. Maybe it is the example in the last section of this chapter, of wanting to lose weight because you feel bad about the way you look. Maybe it is a personal project you'd like to work on, but you feel bad about your ability to create it, like a novel, starting a website, or just writing a letter to a friend you've been putting off. Write down one or more negative thoughts you have about it right now, and why you feel unhappy about it.

Now imagine that you achieve that thing. Write down all the feelings and thoughts you imagine you'll have once you get it done. Can you see the difference in the negativity and positivity? Just noticing that you have these self talk narratives is the point of this exercise.

HOW WE WILL CHANGE YOUR
SELF TALK

In this chapter, we will outline the right mindset you need going into the task of changing your self talk.

When we were growing up, we had teachers, our parents, and other guardians looking out for us. As we learned about the world, we learned what actions were inappropriate, like knocking over our sister's block tower or throwing food, and which were appropriate, like sharing with others or talking in an "inside"-level voice. Our initial reactions and habits were corrected by the people around us. Now, you have to take control and correct yourself. You developed bad habits as a child. And they were corrected and set on a new course. So you can set your current habits on a new course, you'll just have to take the responsibility to recognize the person you are right now and the person you want to become. When we have fallen into negative self talk, the only way for us to notice and correct it is to be responsible for ourselves. If you are ready to take responsibility for your thoughts and actions, keep reading.

Fixed Mindset vs. Growth Mindset

I discussed this first principle in my book on Small Talk, but it is important for self talk, too.

The idea is the fixed mindset vs. the growth mindset. A fixed mindset means that you believe that who you are today is basically who you have always been and who you will always be. When someone has a growth mindset, they acknowledge that they are constantly changing. So someone with a fixed mindset would have self talk that sounds something like, "I can't run this 5k because I am not a runner." A person with a growth mindset would say, "I can run this 5k because I can train." Another example would be, "I can't learn French because I'm bad with languages" as a fixed mindset. The growth mindset would be, "If I put in the effort, I have the capability to learn French, even if it is a skill I find difficult."

Do you see the differences?

As you start to change your self talk, you will need to have the attitude that you possess the capability to change it.

From here forward, you can operate with a mindset of, "I can adapt my thoughts into new patterns, even if it is difficult," instead of, "Changing my thoughts is too hard. This is just how I think and how I am, and how I will always be."

Starting Small: Habit Building

Changing your thoughts will be difficult. Up until now, you've probably not considered your self talk patterns. So being able to be aware of them, and eventually change them, will be a slow-moving process. But you should not give up if it feels hard at first.

Like building any habit, the original patterns feel quite

rigid and stuck. It's like eating fast food every night for dinner and trying to go straight to chicken and vegetables. Changing all at once won't last, and won't be pleasant. But if you slowly start to change your habits, just one day a week, or one food choice at a time, it is easier.

So you will need to break up changing your self talk into smaller habits. A helpful metaphor when we think about changing our thought patterns is imagining that your brain is a forest, and the thought patterns you have are paths you've created over the years. It is easy to walk these paths: The trees are cleared, there are no branches in your way, and it is easy to see each step in front of you. As you try to form a new thought pattern, it is like going off the beaten path and trying to forge a new way. You have to hack at the branches and trees, and progress will be slow, instead of being able to race down the path you already have established. You also don't know the way forward. Which way should you make the path? But once you clear that new path, and walk it over and over, it will become as simple and ingrained as the first one.

It's also just like training your muscles: At first, you can't lift very heavy weights. But as you practice with those weights, then you can move on to heavier and heavier ones, and now your muscles are more defined, and you are stronger. Your brain is a muscle, and at first, you need to start with light weights. Be patient with yourself, and recognize where you are when you begin.

Easily Influenced

You have to believe that you can change. And you *can* change. Our brains and inner chatter, while they can be hard-wired over years and years of repetitive modes of thinking, are also easily influenced.

Have you ever been in the middle of a good book, and after getting lost in the chapters for a few days, you start to think in the pattern of the writing style of the book? Or if you've spent too much of your day on Facebook, you start thinking about life in Facebook statuses? Or if you spent all day looking at spreadsheets, then you have dreams about spreadsheets?

The outside world can heavily influence our inner chatter and thought patterns. All you need to do is make an active effort to contribute to that influence.

Your Self Talk is Yours Alone

One of the best things about changing your inner self talk is that it gets to be your secret. No one needs to know but you about the tactics you use for self talk, as most of them will be hidden inside your brain. Pretty wonderful, yeah? You get to choose how you talk to yourself.

As we move to the next chapter, in which we will begin describing the strategies and steps to change self talk, you may find that some strategies resonate with you and come naturally, while others don't. What's important is that whichever ones work for you, you work on. You may surprised which ones help the most. Try not to judge the strategies before giving them a try. No one has to know you are working on your self talk, it can be your little secret.

You are the boss here. If you are religious and feel most comfortable with religious thoughts that calm you, then go for that. If you enjoy getting woo woo about the universe or mother nature, do that. It's whatever you want. You have my permission to be as silly or as serious as you want.

We have outlined basic strategies to help you find general principles for talking to yourself, but there are a lot of blanks left open based on your particular situation. We'll guide you on HOW to fill them in, but you get to decide the WHAT.

In the next chapter, you'll learn the first step of changing your self talk: awareness.

Exercise: Helpful Habit Building Reminders

Rerouting your thoughts will be a slow process, just like building any habit. At first, it may be hard to remember to step outside of your thoughts and assess them. For this exercise, either use post-it notes or set up reminders on your phone to help you check in with yourself on a daily basis. You can put the post-it notes somewhere around your house where you are likely to see them, like your bathroom mirror, your computer monitor, the visor of your car, wherever you will see the reminder each day. Or, set up reminders on your phone to ping you several times per day to practice your new, positive self talk habit.

THE FIRST STEP IS AWARENESS

The first step to remaking your self talk is to be aware of it. This sounds simple, but can actually be quite difficult when we're lost in a storm of self-criticism, self-doubt, and other negative tendencies that we're so used to we can't even see them.

Like we discussed in the last chapter, building a habit is slow-moving and takes effort. If you didn't do the activity in the last chapter of setting reminders on your phone or setting up post-it notes around your house, you may want to do it now to help you identify self talk.

Make the Monsters Less Scary

Once you can recognize negative self talk, it's like shining a flashlight on a monster creeping around your bedroom in the dark. When you can see it, you realize it's not that scary. Now it has a name, and a shape, and once we see it, we can shoo it out of our bedroom with a broom. We'll get to the "broom" strategies in further chapters, but for now, let's focus on finding our flashlight and using it on that negative self talk.

Once you are able to identify your thoughts, you also gain some distance and perspective on them. Just getting a smidgen of distance from your negative thoughts, even if it doesn't feel like a lot, can make a big difference. Having the room to breathe from overwhelming thoughts makes them less powerful. You may begin to feel relief from your unending negative chatter even just by recognizing the thoughts.

What does recognizing and being aware mean?

When you identify a negative thought, you can label it. We will talk more about naming in a future chapter, but for now, you can use these phrases, or something similar, if you find them helpful:

- I recognize that this is a moment of negativity
- This is stress
- This is uncertainty
- This hurts
- This is a negative thought
- Ouch!

Remember Your Mood

It has been discussed how your mood affects your self-talk, but this is worth repeating again. When you are feeling low, you will be more susceptible to believing your negative self talk and following it wherever it wants to take you. When you are in an upbeat, sunny mood, it will be easier to dismiss negative self talk and think positively.

So awareness also means awareness of mood. Recognize

what mood you are in and how that may be affecting your thinking.

Change Comes Next

Once you have learned to become aware of your negative self talk, the next step will be changing those thoughts. But you can't change them if you can't first find them, so don't rush unless you feel comfortable first identifying your thoughts. Then we will begin the process of change. In the next chapter, we will learn about establishing some distance from your self talk once you have identified it.

Exercise: Writing Down Self Talk

For this chapter about being aware of your negative self talk, you should try to write down a few self talk phrases you use as you notice them throughout the day. Try to write them down verbatim, nailing the exact language and phrasing you use with yourself. It can be anything you notice you say to yourself, and this exercise can be difficult at first, as these thoughts are so ingrained.

YOU ARE NOT YOUR THOUGHTS

I n this chapter, we will learn how to get some distance from our thoughts, and you will realize that you are not your thoughts, even though this may sound scary.

Getting Distance From Your Thoughts

Thinking about thinking is called metacognition. This is a common tactic in philosophy, but it may sound scary if you haven't heard of it before. Basically, in metacognition, you are able to think about your own methods of thinking. You could say that this whole book about your inner monologue, or conversation with yourself, or self talk, is about metacognition.

When you practice metacognition, you realize that you are not your thoughts. If you are able to take a step back from them, you can see that they just pass through your brain and can either get stuck, or you forget them and they continue moving on. A common practice in meditation is to view thoughts as cars passing by. You may be tempted to chase after good thoughts and stop bad ones, but practicing metacognition means just watching them going by, and trying not to judge them. Eventually, we will get to retraining your thought patterns for better thoughts, but for now, just realizing that you are not your thoughts is enough. It may be difficult to get a grasp on, but just spend some time thinking about this, however redundant that may sound.

One way to realize that your thoughts are outside of you is to say them out loud, and label them as thoughts. If you are feeling a bit overwhelmed by the amount of work you have to do, you may think: "This is too much, and I don't know how I'll get everything finished." But you can distance yourself from this thought by thinking, "I'm having a thought that this work is too much and won't get finished."

Even though identifying it as a thought or feeling seems like a small difference, it makes a big difference.

Where Does Self Talk Come From?

Where do the thoughts in our self talk patterns come from?

Are you the source of your negative self talk? Did you come up with this stuff, or did someone else? Investigate your negative self talk thoughts and think about where you first heard them. Were you influenced by pop culture or a TV show? Or someone in your family? The bully in middle school? Your mom? Figure out where they come from. Knowing the source helps to question their validity. Sometimes others criticize us for what they don't like about themselves; they put their insecurities onto us. Don't take on the cruel insecurities of others.

Your thoughts could also come from your limiting beliefs. You may need to look at the root cause, deep down of your negative self talk. Maybe your negative self talk is that you are lazy because you don't go the gym at least four times per week. You are telling yourself you are lazy, but what is the limiting belief deep down that keeps you in this negative loop? Maybe the belief is that you don't deserve to take some time for yourself, to better your health. And you believe this because the last relationship you were in, your partner didn't like it when you did things without him or her. So you feel guilty taking time for yourself. So your negative self talk comes from a different place, from your feelings about how much time you deserve for yourself.

You may find that some of your internal self talk is not true or accurate, but just something someone else has said or that you got from somewhere else. Remember, this chapter is about the fact that you are not your thoughts. Even if your thoughts tell you that you are your thoughts, they are wrong! Don't believe them! You can assess your thoughts to determine if they hold water or not. If they don't, you can change them, and in the next chapter we will look at ways to investigate whether a negative thought is true or not.

Exercise: Where Did the Phrase Originate From?

For the exercise for this chapter, choose a self talk phrase you wrote down in last chapter's exercise, and see if you can figure out where it originated from. Do you know how long you have been telling yourself this thought? Do you remember where you first heard it? Does it come from someone else, or from a deeper belief you hold about yourself or your approach to life?

QUESTIONING A NEGATIVE THOUGHT

I n this chapter we will look at how to "interrogate" a negative thought, as if you have sat it down in a single-bulb interrogation room and are getting ready to find out the truth from this pesky negative self talk. First, we'll look at "parking" your thoughts, and then we'll get to the questions you can use to analyze them.

"Parking" a Thought

The first step in interrogating your negative self talk thought is to get it into the interrogation room. Earlier, we spoke about the metaphor of your mind being a crowded street. The thoughts are cars racing by, and some of them are good, some of them bad. So to interrogate a thought, we first have to "pull it over," or "park" it.

What that means is simple: You just become aware enough of the thought, maybe even writing it down, to stop it in its tracks for some assessment. As discussed in the previous chapters, that isn't always easy, but that doesn't mean it can't be done. All you need is a little practice to become familiar with recognizing your negative thoughts to park them.

So, once you've effectively parked a thought, the next step is the interrogation. We will look at some questions you can ask your thought to assess its validity.

Interrogating a Thought

OK, let's get down to the good stuff: Let's see just how true that negative self talk thought you're having is.

Once you identify a negative thought you are having about a situation or yourself, you can break it down and deconstruct it.

ASK YOURSELF:

- Who is this important to?
- How much does this matter in the long run?
- Is my response an overreaction?
- Am I overgeneralizing?
- What is the concrete evidence for this thought?
- Am I viewing things in terms of absolutes? (Remember the "polarizing" type of negative self talk from the first chapter.)
- Should it be more of a gray area?
- Am I assuming the thoughts or feelings of others?
- Am I using cruel language?
- If I were having a positive thought about this, how would I interpret things?
- What is the worst thing that could result from

this? How likely is that to actually happen? If it did happen, what would be the next step I would take?

- Could the situation or feeling be worse?
- Is this thinking going to help me achieve my goals?
- What would help me feel better or think a different way?
- What can I learn from this thought?
- What is another way to interpret the situation? What would that mean?
- What physical evidence for this exists, and how much is my feeling or perception?
- What is the evidence for my conclusion?
- How would a friend talk to me about this thought?
- How would someone from a different culture or upbringing feel about this thought?
- If I am ruminating on a choice I made in the past, am I prepared to take steps to make a change right now? Otherwise I need to let it go. But if I am willing to make change, then I need to take those steps.

Interrogating a Thought: Example

As an example, I will show you how I might break down a negative self talk thought with these questions:

NEGATIVE SELF TALK: *I am a failure because I am single.*

- Who is this important to? *Being single is important to me. I'd like to share my life with someone. But it seems more important to my parents, who want me to be married like my brother and sister. Maybe it is more important to them, actually.*
- How much does this matter in the long run? *I want to eventually get married, so it matters in the long run. But I guess in "the long run" I have more time to find a partner.*
- Is my response an overreaction? *I have other areas of my life I feel successful in. My career is going well.*
- Am I overgeneralizing? Does my thought apply to everyone who is similar in this way to me? *Is everyone who is single a failure? No, there are a lot of people who choose to be single or are happy being single.*
- What is the concrete evidence for this thought? *I feel bad when I go to family gatherings without a partner. But those are my feelings. My parents always ask when I'm getting married. So their question is evidence that they think I'm a failure. No, it is concrete evidence that they want me to have a partner.*
- Am I viewing things in terms of absolutes? (Remember the "polarizing" type of negative self talk from the first chapter.) *Yes. I am defining myself as a failure because I am single.*
- Should it be more of a gray area? *Yes. I am not an absolute failure in every area of life, I guess.*
- Am I assuming the thoughts or feelings of others? *I am assuming that my parents think I'm a failure because they allude to wanting me to have a partner.*

- Am I using cruel language? *Failure is pretty harsh.*
- If I were having a positive thought about this, how would I interpret things? *I have a lot of time to pursue my own interests being single, and maybe I am doing so well at work because I don't have to worry about making extra time for a partner right now.*
- What is the worst thing that could result from this? How likely is that to actually happen? If it did happen, what would be the next step I would take? *The worst thing that could happen is that I stay single forever. It could happen but it seems everyone finds someone at some point, so there is a chance I will find a partner. If I did end up single forever, the next step I would take is maybe adopting a child on my own.*
- Could the situation or feeling be worse? *Yes. I could be "older" with "less time" to find a partner. My grandma even found a new boyfriend at the nursing home a few years after my grandpa died. I have had dating experience before, it would be harder to date without my previous experience. I could live in a small town, instead of this big city, where there are more opportunities for dating.*
- Is this thinking going to help me achieve my goals? *Thinking I am a failure probably won't attract a partner.*
- What would help me feel better or think a different way? *I could try to not feel so ashamed about being single. Maybe then I'd put myself out there more for dating.*
- What can I learn from this thought? *I can learn*

that being single is a sore spot for me and something I'm sensitive about. Probably because my parents put pressure on me.

- What is another way to interpret the situation? What would that mean? *Maybe I am less of a "failure" than my friends who got married too young and are already divorced. Though it's not nice to think of my friends as failures. That means if it's not nice to call them failures, it's not nice to call myself a failure.*

- What physical evidence for this exists, and how much is my feeling or perception? *I can't think of any physical evidence. I don't have a ring on my finger? That seems like a silly reason to be a failure, not wearing a piece of jewelry on a certain finger.*

- What is the evidence for my conclusion? *I guess there is no evidence, I just don't like going to events with friends where I know everyone will be a couple except me.*

- How would a friend talk to me about this thought? *A friend would probably tell me I need to date more and am not putting myself out there enough if I am not happy being single.*

- How would someone from a different culture or upbringing feel about this thought? *I guess some people have arranged marriages in other cultures and would probably want to be single like me.*

- If I am ruminating on a choice I made in the past, am I prepared to take steps to make a change right now? Otherwise I need to let it go. But if I am willing to make change, then I need to take those steps. *I sometimes wish I hadn't broken up*

*with my boyfriend and imagine what our life would
be like still together. But I don't want to get back with
him, as our relationship was not good. So, no, I am
not willing to make a change, so I should stop
wasting time daydreaming about not having broken
up with him. I should focus on the future instead.*

THAT IS JUST one example of a way to interrogate a thought. The questions are very open-ended, so whatever direction your answers take you is fine. Just try to be as honest with yourself as possible and not let the negative thought win. Negative thoughts can be very powerful, and you may have to play a bit of "bad cop" with them, treating them as if they were hostile witnesses. Of course, that's just a fun metaphor, and you shouldn't be extremely critical of your own thoughts, as that is only furthering your negativity. We will talk about that in a later chapter, but for now, just try to assess your thoughts honestly and without judgment. In the next chapter, we'll look at the "Opposite Thought" strategy for turning around our self talk.

Exercise: Interrogate a Thought

For the exercise for this chapter, choose a thought and interrogate it using some or all of the questions found in this chapter. Your answers do not need to be long, but you can go as in-depth as you want. You may discover something revealing about where your negative thoughts are coming from or how they are holding you back, but also don't spend hours and hours on this task for a single thought, as that could be seen as rumination. Spend maybe 20 minutes on average to go through the list. You also don't need to write your answers down, but can just do them in your head. This will be good practice for positive and realistic self talk, too.

THE OPPOSITE THOUGHT

Now that you know how to interrogate your negative self talk, we will move on to how you can reshape that negative talk into something more positive. The strategies in this chapter will revolve around an old tactic we all remember from childhood: The Opposite Game.

Thinking Opposites

When we have negative self talk, one of the easiest strategies to use to try to flip our thoughts around is to think: *What is the opposite of what I've just thought about myself or this situation?*

For example, if you think, "Today is a crappy day because I forgot to send an important email this morning," just play a game with yourself where you think of the opposite thought. What would the opposite of this thought be? There is not one correct "opposite" answer, like "black is the opposite of white." The possibilities for opposite thoughts are infinite. Let's find a few based around the idea of why today is the opposite of a "crappy day:" Why it is a "great day."

- Today is a great day because I have a job
- Today is a great day because I have learned a valuable lesson about setting reminders for my most important tasks
- Today is a great day because I had a nice lunch with a new coworker
- Today is a great day because I am alive

YOU CAN MAKE it as small as a good sandwich or as large as appreciating that you get to be alive. As long as the opposite thought is positive or realistic, it is the opposite of your negative thought.

Let's try another one: "I don't like my body." Just challenge yourself and your original position you are coming from. Each time you challenge yourself, you are making that new pathway through the forest, or building the new habits and thought patterns in your mind.

So if you are unhappy with your body, what are some amazing things your body allows you to do?

- Your eyes allow you to see a beautiful sunset.
- Your feet allow you to walk down the street.
- Your brain allows you to read or watch TV, activities you find pleasurable.
- Your nerves and skin allow you to feel the touch

of another person, whether it is romantic or just
a hug from a friend

- Your ears allow you to hear a song you like

So REMEMBER, the opposite strategy is as simple as asking yourself, what's the opposite of that thought I just had? It could be the key to reevaluating your approach to the world and your life. You can be as creative as you like.

Recognize Your Strengths

When thinking of opposite thoughts, it is often important to recognize our own strengths. Of course, your strengths should actually be your strengths. They should be grounded in reality. Even if you feel down on yourself, we all have unique or good things about us that we can think about during a low point.

In the exercise for this chapter, you will write a list of your strengths.

It is also important to remember that even if something feels like a weakness for you, it is probably not as bad as you think.

For example, let's say you feel nervous about meeting new people, and you feel like you always make a poor first impression.

You may think, "I am not good at meeting new people."

(If this sounds like you, you may also enjoy my book on improving your social skills called "Small Talk: How to Talk to People, Improve Your Charisma, Social Skills, Conversation Starters & Lessen Social Anxiety.")

While this may feel true, you can think of a more positive thought, one that is more "growth mindset" rather than "fixed mindset." We are all always changing, and we do not have to be stuck as defined as one thing for our whole lives.

So, the opposite thought of "I am not good at meeting new people" wouldn't be "I am great at meeting new people," as it's probably not true for you. But you can think:

- "I am working on improving my social skills."
- "I am proud of myself for getting out of my comfort zone to meet new people, when it is an activity I recognize makes me nervous."
- "I am grateful I only feel that my skills could improve for meeting new people, and that I don't have a fear of leaving my house or diagnosed anxiety, which I imagine would be worse."

Watch Your Language

When constructing your opposite statements, it is helpful to avoid absolute statements.

Avoid words like "always" or "never." You don't have to be 100% or 0%, and in fact, nothing in life is that way. (Well, almost nothing.) If you don't get to the gym one day, you may think "I always screw up my workout routine," and then write off the whole week. Instead, just think, "I made a mistake here, and I am learning from this mistake and others I've made in the past." Don't forget to also look at the days you did make it to the gym. Let's say you want to get to the gym 3 days per week. If you miss 1 day, and only go 2 days out of the week, you may only ruminate on the 1 day you missed. But try to focus on wins, as well: "I made it to the gym 2 days this week. That's 2 more days that I would have gone 4 months ago, before I started being more conscious of my health." That's a huge win!

Don't get complacent, remember to learn from why you didn't hit your goal, but don't forget to focus on the positives.

You can also pay attention to the language you use to see whether it is neutral or judgmental. You can replace very negative statements that have cruel, judgmental language with more neutral language.

"I am fat," becomes "My body is bigger than I'd like it to be."

"I am a lazy worker," becomes "I could improve my focus at work."

"I feel stupid in meetings with my boss," becomes, "I feel unprepared for my meetings with my boss."

Do you see the difference? Take out judgmental, mean words like "fat," "lazy" and "stupid," from the way you talk to yourself, and replace them with less cruel words to describe yourself to yourself in your self talk.

These small changes in language seem like minor details, but the difference they can make is huge.

In the next chapter, we will look at gaining perspective when we have overwhelmingly negative self talk.

Exercise: Identify Your Strengths

In the exercise for this chapter, write down a list of your strengths. If you are feeling down on yourself, even coming up with one strength to focus on can make you feel a lot better. If you are having trouble coming up with your strengths, ask a friend or family member for help. Other people are often better at being positive about us than we are ourselves.

PERSPECTIVE

W e've already practiced taking a step back from thoughts and dis-identifying with them. Now we will practice taking a step back even from ourselves, to focus on others and get some perspective about our place in the world.

Think About Others

When you are suffering from negative self talk, it can feel like your problems are huge, as big as elephants stampeding through your living room, destroying everything in sight. How will you pick up all the pieces and carry on?

You can feel heavy, or like you are carrying a lot with you, like the saying "carrying the weight of the world on his shoulders." But one tactic you can use to ease this weight is to think about that world you feel like you are carrying.

You can focus your energy on others. This strategy can be helpful when you're throwing yourself a pity party. Everyone likes a pity party, when it's thrown just for one. But if you were to invite everyone in your social circles, it might quickly turn uncomfortable. You wouldn't want those people feeling bad for you, right? They probably all feel bad at some time or another, and they know what this feeling is like. Everyone has some negative thought patterns. Thinking about the lives and concerns of others can make us feel not so alone, and feel better, comparatively, to the problems of others. It's not about comparison, though. It's just about getting a quick dose of perspective when feeling down.

If you are feeling bad about your position in your company, for example, you may be comparing yourself to a friend with a seemingly impressive job title and high-powered career. But what if you know of another friend who is stressed about losing his or her job? You cannot always compare yourself to others you feel are doing better than you. To make this fair and realistic, you should also spend equal time thinking about people who are worse-off than you. Even if you don't feel you have an impressive job title, at least you are not worried about losing your job.

It is also important to recognize that suffering is a part of life. It is common to all of humanity, and you are not alone in your feelings and self-criticism. However, though everyone struggles, we all could do to struggle a little less. We have enough outside obstacles to overcome; why give ourselves more grief by adding to them with negative self talk? As you are learning in this book, changing your approach to the thoughts you tell yourself can ease that common suffering of humanity a little bit.

Laugh at Yourself

Another way to gain some perspective about the negative self talk you have about yourself and your life is to remember that life can be pretty absurd. Humor is a good antidote.

What feels a bit silly or funny to one person will not always resonate with someone else's funny bone, but whatever helps you cope and get some levity and distance from swirling negative thoughts can be yours to enjoy.

For example, if you're feeling a bit self-conscious at the gym, and it makes it hard for you to show up and get your butt off the couch, you can try to think about how absurd the idea of a gym is. Humans evolved fighting for survival in the African plains. Way back when, people didn't eat for days at a time, had to hunt, and struggled to put enough calories in their body that they would expend on a taxing hunt, often while going hungry. Today, humans are pretty comfortable, comparably. So comfortable, in fact, that we build big boxes with machines of varying movements just to exercise our rested bodies. What would cave people think of the muscled and toned people who spend so much time at the gym to make their body look a certain way? It's a bit absurd if you take a step back from it. That can give you just a little boost of confidence and a "who cares" attitude to get to the gym and not feel so intimidated.

It is worth mentioning again that all the strategies in this book are meant to help you, but you can cherry-pick which ones work for you and which ones don't.

People are Self-Focused

The last tactic to help you gain some perspective over your negative self talk is to ask yourself: Who cares?

Often, it is only you, and the extremely high standards you set for yourself. When we set ourselves up to fail, negative self talk can run rampant. Give your inner critic a day off sometimes. If you don't care, does anyone? (Of course, don't take this to the extreme of not caring about anything in your life. But it is OK to relax a bit sometimes instead of always being so negative and harsh on yourself. You may even find that being a bit kinder to yourself does wonders to your performance in areas you want to improve. But that is what we will get to in another chapter.)

When you think about "Who cares?" you can also remember that everyone is more focused on themselves than they are on anyone else. Aren't you reading a book about the way you talk to yourself inside your head? That we all have these constant thoughts should tell you a lot about how self-focused people are.

If you are having negative self thoughts about an impression you made or something embarrassing you feel you've done, the people you felt embarrassed in font of probably don't remember it as well as you do, or weren't thinking about you, but were in fact thinking about themselves.

Remembering that people are often worrying about themselves can take some of the pressure off of you.

In the next chapter, we will look at a few different ways to talk to yourself with different labels or names.

Exercise

For this exercise, choose either the strategy of thinking of others or the strategy of humor for one of your self talk thoughts. Assess the thought by thinking of others, or by taking a step back and enjoying the absurdity of life.

OUTSIDE INFLUENCES TO CONSIDER

T hough we have, in previous chapters, looked at how changing our external circumstances won't change our internal dialogue with ourselves, there are three areas of your life that I believe will help you considerably in your journey towards a healthier life and healthier self talk. We will look at meditation, health and friends.

Meditation

Meditation and mindfulness, as I will use them here, are interchangeable terms. You may have heard of one or both of them before. While meditation has been around for thousands of years, mindfulness has only entered the popular lexicon recently.

Both traditions mean having more awareness of your body, your mind and your thoughts. If you want to take up a formal meditation practice, you can start by sitting quietly and trying to notice your thoughts and not becoming attached to them for just 5 or 10 minutes a day. There are a number of beginner apps out there for your phone if you think this will be helpful to you.

You can also start practicing more meditation and mindfulness by focusing on your breath when you are in a stressful situation or feeling extremely emotional. Taking just 5 deep breaths will give you the space you need, will help calm down your nervous system, and will give you a break before you react emotionally and quickly to something.

Another technique is to just take a break to notice your surroundings or your thoughts when going about your day. Whether you are walking to work, driving, sitting at your computer, eating a meal, or talking to a friend, focus on what you can see, hear, smell, touch or taste. How do your hands feel on the steering wheel? What is your friend saying? Listen intently. How does each individual flavor taste? How do they work together? Being more present in the immediate moment can also help you to feel calmer and more aware of your thoughts and experiences.

Overall, just taking pause throughout your day can greatly improve your own mental chatter. I think you will find that some mindfulness in your life will help you greatly reroute the patterns of self talk you have built in your mind.

Diet & Exercise

Another factor that I believe can have a big impact on changing your inner self talk is taking care of your body. While many people find they have a lot of negative self talk around these very topics, working towards them can give you a big leg up in rerouting your brain patterns.

The idea behind the mind-body connection is that the

health of our minds and our bodies is closely linked. By putting healthy food into your body and moving it around with at least some light exercise a few days a week, you keep your brain in the best health possible as well. Start with small goals, like just putting on your gym shoes to go get the mail. You may find you end up walking around the block. Or just choosing the side salad instead of a side of fries with a juicy burger.

Taking care of our bodies goes a long way toward taking care of our mental health.

Social Circle

The last external factor that I think makes a big difference toward our inner monologues is surrounding ourselves with people who also have healthy and more positive-leaning thought patterns. There is a saying that you are the average of the 5 people you spend the most time with. Being around positive people will naturally make you more positive. When you talk to yourself negatively less often, and become more aware of it, you will probably become more aware of how the people around you talk negatively. You may find that you naturally don't enjoy being around people you didn't notice were so negative before.

Meditation, health and social circles are three external factors that can help you make the thought patterns in your brain healthier, more positive and more constructive.

Exercise: Exercise!

For this chapter's exercise, take one step toward bettering one area from this chapter. Call a positive friend to grab coffee and catch up. Meditate for 10 minutes. Go for a walk, or to the gym, or eat vegetables with dinner tonight. Make one small change that you can claim as a "win" in the area of meditation, health or social circles.

CONCLUSION

Thank you for reading "Self Talk," and I hope you have learned something from this short book. The relationship we have with ourselves is the longest and most guaranteed one we will experience our entire lives. We can never escape ourselves, so we might as well make ourselves into our best friends and biggest supporters. I truly believe that begins with positive self talk. Too many people are too harsh on themselves, and I think we could all benefit from more kindness and positivity in our lives toward ourselves.

If you have followed along in these chapters and performed the exercises, you are well on your way to a healthier inner life. Changing your self talk isn't easy, and can be a life-long journey. Continue to reference this book for strategies to help you with your own inner self talk, and go slow as you build new, happier thoughts and habits.

I hope you enjoyed reading this book and that you found it helpful to you.

Sincerely,

Aston

PART II

SELF CARE

LOVE YOURSELF: HOW TO EMBRACE
SELF-COMPASSION, BODY LOVE & SELF
LOVE FOR LIFE-CHANGING WELLNESS &
SELF-ESTEEM

SELF CARE: LOVE YOURSELF

HOW TO EMBRACE SELF COMPASSION, BODY LOVE & SELF LOVE FOR LIFE-CHANGING WELLNESS & SELF ESTEEM

ASTON SANDERSON

INTRODUCTION

Dear Reader,

Welcome to *Self-Care*, a short guide that will help you live your best life through taking care of the most important person in your life: YOU.

The subtitle for this book is, *How to Embrace Self-Compassion, Body Love and Self Love for Life-Changing Wellness and Self-Esteem*. This subtitle means that we'll be exploring a few different ideas of just what self-care can be. Self-care can mean a lot of different things to different people, and this book will offer you insight into a few different methods of applying self-care:

- **Self-Compassion:** This means feeling an empathy and sympathy toward yourself. This is self-care through **emotions and the spiritual.**
- **Body Love:** This means taking care of yourself **physically.** Often, when we are being self-destructive in our lives, the first thing to go is our physical health, whether that means not

exercising, eating junk foods, or not taking time
to chill out and relax physically.

- **Self-Love:** In this category, we group together
several more kinds of self-care: in the **mental and
social** realms.

What does "Life-Changing Wellness and Self-Esteem"
mean? This means that when you put the exercises and
theories in this book into practice, you will experience a
transformation in your life.

A word of caution, though: often, in our present-day
society, transformation is sold as a quick-fix. It's just something you can capture in a bottle and buy over-the-counter.
All you need is to read one book, or take one course, and
voilà! All your dreams have come true. Unfortunately, that's
not how real life works.

So, in this book, I'm not telling you that all you need to
do is read this short guide, and overnight you'll be a new
you. Applying the concepts in this book will be challenging
at first. You are taking the first step on a long journey, and
I'm not promising it will be easy. But, if you do put in the
work, you'll find that the rewards are ten-fold. This is some
of the most important work you can do for yourself, for
those around you, and for the world. Yes, taking care of
yourself is *generous,* not *selfish*. This will be an important
point we'll explore further in this book.

If you've found this book, you may be feeling stressed,
overwhelmed, exhausted, and frustrated. Maybe you don't
know what to do to solve your problems. Maybe you're not
sleeping at night, you constantly feel anxious, or you're
running around like a chicken with its head cut off.

Take a deep breath.

We'll get through this together.

This guide will help you fight those feelings and replace them with more positive ones. Follow this guide, and you'll be thankful you did.

I'd like to point out that this book is **quite short**. If you want a 300-page book, by all means, find one! But I haven't stuffed this book with filler. *Self-care* gets straight to the point, because I respect your time. I know you're stressed and really feeling that stress, otherwise you wouldn't have made it this far into the introduction! (Or, maybe you are feeling OK, but just want to feel even better. I welcome those readers, too. You'll also find this book helpful.)

So, I've made this book as short and jam-packed as possible. I hope you enjoy that and get a feeling of satisfaction from being able to finish reading it quickly.

There are **end-of-chapter activities** for each section of this book. You may want to move on to a new chapter only after completing the activity, or you may decide that you want to read the entire book and then come back and pick and choose which activities to do, and in what order. Either method is fine, but I do encourage you to walk away from this book having **completed at least one activity** from it.

If you can implement just one practical change in your life from this book, my job will have been complete. Of course, I hope this book I've worked so hard to put together for you accomplishes much more than just one change for you. Readers of my previous books, like *Small Talk* and *Self Talk* have written me to say the books have changed their lives, and they've revisited the books as reference guides many times. I hope you will be able to say the same.

Lastly, I'd like to point out that I am not a medical professional, and the advice in this book does not stand in for medical advice, should you need it. If you are feeling clinically depressed, or in a bad mental state which you're finding hard to climb out of yourself, please contact someone to help you. Maybe ask a friend for help first, if you're afraid of seeking out a mental health professional on your own.

OK, now that you have an introduction to the concept of self-care and what this book will hopefully teach you, let's get started. In the first chapter, we'll discuss what exactly self-care is, in our definition.

Are you ready? Let's dive in!

— Aston Sanderson, Author

WHAT IS SELF-CARE?

W hat is "self-care"?
        Maybe self-care seems vague and impractical. We've all heard the term "self-care" before, but if you're like most people, you may have never had it defined for you.

In this first chapter, we'll define exactly what self-care means as we use it in this book.

It turns out self-care can mean many different things, but to me, that isn't a negative. That just means that there are many different facets of self-care to explore, and whichever ones resonate with you most are the ones you can adopt for yourself.

Let's dive in to some important aspects of self-care:

A BASIC DEFINITION

A basic definition of self-care is that it's anything you do —mentally or physically—to be kind or nurturing to yourself. That's anything from watching Netflix to unwind (though we'll explore that more deeply in the chapter "Getting Unplugged"), to taking a walk, to repeating an affirmation, such as, "I am a good person" in your mind.

Let's explore some more facets of self-care below.

Self-Care is Under Your Control

OK, you're thinking, this is SO obvious. But this aspect of self-care is crucial and cannot be glossed over.

A very important aspect of approaching your self-care journey is having a Growth Mindset instead of a Fixed Mindset. A growth mindset means you believe it is possible to grow and change. A fixed mindset means you believe there are things about yourself that are just black-and-white true.

Let's look at some examples:

Fixed Mindset: "I am bad at learning languages."

Growth Mindset: "I can improve at learning new languages if I put in the work."

Although you started with a rigid idea about yourself that limited your options (you wouldn't even try learning Italian), when you changed your mindset, you suddenly opened a *whole new world of possibilities* for yourself—a new world where you could learn Italian, if you tried.

So how does this relate to self-care? You may have some fixed mindset ideas about self-care, like:

"I just don't have time to take care of myself."

"There are more important things in my life to worry about than me."

"I'm bad at relaxing."

Growth mindset ideas allow for change:

"I can find the time to take care of myself if I get creative with my time management."

"I can learn how to take care of other important things in my life by taking care of me."

"I can learn how to relax better."

So, remember: self-care is under your control.

The biggest block to taking care of yourself isn't your time, or your money, or your prior commitments: it's YOU.

The first step to self-care is believing it's possible to change, to do the work of self-care, to feel better. Take control of your self-care mindset, and you'll be amazed by the things you can achieve.

SELF-CARE IS Preventative

Self-care isn't just for de-stressing after a tough day at the office. It isn't only about reacting to stress or negative feelings after they happen, but taking the time to prevent those negative feelings in the first place.

For example, let's say you have a big presentation coming up at work. You could give in to your stressed-out, I'm-freaking-out, nervous feelings in the weeks leading up the presentation, and then book a mini vacation for yourself the weekend after it's done.

But you know what might be better? Booking that weekend getaway the weekend before the presentation. I know, that sounds absolutely crazy. How could you ever find the time? But, if you know you have a small no-work vacation planned, you'll actually find the time to meet your goals ahead of time. Have you ever heard the principle, "Work expands to fill the time allowed for it"? You can do the same amount of work on the presentation—in less time.

And then, when you do take the weekend away right before the presentation, you'll be able to ground yourself. Connect with yourself and who you are away from all the craziness of your job (which, by the way, is not WHO you are!). Allowing for this grounding and connection will give you the perspective to realize your presentation is not The Most Important Thing in the World (which will calm your nerves). In the end it will help you to perform *better* on your presentation.

Pretty wild concept, huh? So, remember that self-care is preventative.

Self-Care is **Restorative**

OK, yes, I will admit, self-care is also restorative. Life, of course, is not predictable. It moves along in ways we never could have expected, and sometimes we'll wake up and realize we are stressed, overwhelmed and stretched too thin, and we have no idea how we got there.

That's perfectly fine, and normal. It happens to all of us more often than we'd like. Even the most preventative self-care can't always take the unknown into account.

So, yes, sometimes self-care means you had the crummiest week and you just need to don sweatpants, get your favorite comfort food and cry. This is a cliché move, but this can be a form of self-care. There may be some reasons you'd be better off putting on real pants, eating a healthy meal, and, OK, maybe still crying at some point. But we'll discuss that in later chapters.

Self-Care is **Deliberate**

Self-care isn't accidental. You can't say that you'll just make sure to be nice to yourself this week and then expect it to happen. You have to think it through: what will you do for self-care? Why? And then you need to schedule it in and actually do it.

A lot of things you do already in your life may be forms of self-care. Things like meeting up with a good friend, treating yourself to a new gadget or ice cream cone occasionally, journaling, or listening to music. You may not recognize them as self-care right now, and that's fine. Part of reading this book means discovering your self-care plan and what self-care means to you, and then being purposeful about self-care in your life.

Even if you read this book and realize you're doing a spectacular job with self-care, you'll at least be more aware of it and thoughtful about it after going through this guide.

Self-Care is Self-Initiated and Directed

Well, it has "self" in the title, doesn't it? Here's another definition that may seem a bit obvious. This goes hand-in-hand with self-care being a deliberate practice you put into place.

Though it would be nice, we can't outsource the responsibility of self-care to someone else. Even if you're doing well enough financially to have your assistant book you in a weekly massage, you still need to decide if that is the best form of self-care for you. (Because as you'll learn in later chapters, what we often think of as relaxation—the aforementioned sweatpants, a massage—are actually not super helpful for taking care of ourselves.)

So, self-care is *your* job. But this is actually quite freeing. You don't need to call a meeting. You don't need to check with others. (OK, maybe your spouse or partner if it means rescheduling something for the family so you can get some alone time.) But you are the boss here. And if you need some time away, hopefully the people in your life understand you're doing what's best for you and will accommodate you.

Self-Care is Medicinal, Spiritual, Mental, Physical and Philosophical

Self-care, in medical terms, might mean putting a Band-Aid on a cut yourself, without a medical professional's help. In philosophy, self-care might mean coming to an understanding of a greater sense of self.

In this book, self-care has many different facets: spiritual, emotional, physical, mental, and yes, medicinal and philosophical, too.

We'll go more into these types of self-care in the next chapter, but for now, just know that whatever specific area of your life in which you need self-care right now, that's the area you can focus on as you go through this book.

What Isn't Self-Care?

Self-care *isn't* selfish. We'll have a whole chapter explaining why that's true later on in this book. But when you take care of yourself, that actually means you'll have greater energy and emotional and mental capacity to care for others. So if you want to help others, help yourself first.

Self-care also isn't *indulgent*. People may think taking time for themselves is a waste of time or energy, but it is necessary. Everyone needs some time that's just for them. After all, relationships, jobs, homes, etc. will all come and go throughout the course of your life, but you'll have a relationship with yourself from Day 1 until the end. So you better make sure it's a good one!

We've gone over a few definitions and important aspects of self-care in this chapter, so you should have a greater idea of what you're getting into, what self-care means in general, and which aspects of self-care resonate most with you.

IN THE NEXT CHAPTER, we'll dive deeper into the different types of self-care, drilling down from vague ideas about the topic and getting more practical and literal for your everyday life.

ACTIVITY

For this chapter, your activity will be very easy, to get you on a roll with the other end-of-chapter activities. For this activity, choose which attribute of self-care with which you most identify. For example, choose a bolded subject heading like "Self-Care is Deliberate" or "Self-Care is Self-Initiated."

Write this definition on a post-it note, scrap piece of paper, old receipt, whatever! And use this as your bookmark for your book. If you're reading on a Kindle or e-reader (or your phone), put the note in a place where you are likely to see it each day. Maybe this is your bedroom nightstand or your bathroom mirror. Just put it somewhere where you will be reminded of this aspect of self-care that most appeals to you.

This activity will urge you to spend more time thinking about self-care. And when you have an easy definition of one aspect of self-care to remember, it will stick in your head. So, take 30 seconds to scratch out this message and put it somewhere to help keep self-care forefront in your mind.

TYPES OF SELF-CARE

In this chapter, we'll delve into different kinds of self-care. Self-care activities can fall into different types, and you may find that certain categories resonate more with you than others. That's OK. Trying to focus on all of them at once, and going from 'zero-to-60' may leave you feeling more burned out than when you started! And that's the opposite of self-care. So, for now, just see which ones spark a bit of interest for you, or which categories you know you need to work on in your own self-care.

Let's look at the self-care categories.

EMOTIONAL

Self-care that is emotion-based is focused on your feelings. Sometimes we can let our emotions overwhelm us and drive us. But focusing too much on controlling your emotions with an iron fist is also a recipe for disaster. A happy medium or balance with your emotions is key.

When you do emotional self-care, this is anything that puts you in touch with your inner emotions more deeply, or that affects your mood. Examples of emotional self-care are journaling about your feelings, writing thank you notes to connect more deeply with gratitude, or having a good cry if you need it.

SENSORY

Sensory self-care is about being mindful and connecting more deeply with your surroundings. These self-care activities will relate to the five senses: touch, taste, sight, smell and sound. This may mean eating a favorite chocolate to delight in the sense of rich taste, going on a walk in nature to pay attention to the light cascading through the trees or the sounds of the birds, or simply lighting your favorite-smelling candle and taking in the aroma.

This type of self-care can be very helpful for brining you back to the present moment. Often, when we're overwhelmed and stressed, our thoughts swirl around our brain at a rapid pace and we can't seem to get control or slow them down.

Sensory self-care brings us back into our body and slows our thoughts by slowing our awareness. When you are focusing on the smell of your favorite candle, it is much harder to think about everything you need to do next week.

PHYSICAL

Physical self-care can be related to sensory self-care, as they both focus on the body. But whereas sensory self-care focuses on the five senses, physical self-care is more about body love, or treating our bodies as temples, as the saying goes. Examples of physical self-care could be getting a massage, going for a run, stretching or doing yoga, or having a soothing bubble bath.

This type of self-care helps us to ground ourselves in the present moment by paying attention to our bodies and showing love for them. Sometimes we believe our bodies are separate from our minds, but everything is interconnected. Why do we get sick when we are feeling stressed? Why do we feel like we have tons of energy when we're excited about something, even if we didn't sleep very much last night? It's because of the mind-body connection. Our minds and bodies are interlinked more than we know, and the simple act of caring for your body has a calming effect on the mind.

This is a very gentle and loving form of self-care, but one with which people sometimes struggle. They might not feel they deserve to treat their bodies well, but that is a topic we'll discuss in a further chapter.

SPIRITUAL

Spiritual self-care relates to emotional self-care, but expands our area of focus from the self and the emotions to the whole world, the universe, and higher beings. Whether you follow a specific religion or not, spiritual self-care is important. Examples of this activity could be praying, meditating, or visiting a religious service or monument. No matter what specifically makes you feel spiritual and connected to a powerful force outside yourself, taking the time to identify something meaningful to you will bring huge dividends.

Finding our place in this world and having perspective is a great force for self-care.

.   .   .

SOCIAL

Social self-care is one of my personal favorites. Often, when I'm feeling in a rut, the last thing I want to do is go out and see people. But afterward, I always feel a thousand times better than before. Even if I dread it, a social situation forces me to share a bit of myself with people and to receive their contribution to our relationship back.

Social doesn't have to mean attending a giant party. It could just be calling, emailing, or texting a friend. Though nothing can replace in-person communication and togetherness, sometimes we just need to know there's someone else out there who cares about us.

MENTAL

The last form of self-care is mental self-care. This means finding something to challenge your brain and stoke your curiosity. Examples of mental self-care are doing the crossword, reading a book, or taking a cooking class to learn something new.

Mental self-care is great for us because when we are focusing on learning a new skill or concentrating on solving a puzzle, this takes over our working memory, and we can no longer focus on how down we are feeling. Finishing a sudoku puzzle or a book also gives us a great feeling of having done something productive.

These are the different types of self-care: emotional, sensory, physical, spiritual, social, and mental. You should now have a better understanding of what each of these types of self-care mean, and so in the next chapter, we'll delve into a huge list of examples of each.

. . .

ACTIVITY

The activity for this chapter is to identify which area of self-care most appeals to you. Though drawing from each category at different times makes for a well-rounded self-care routine, for now, don't bite off more than you can chew —just focus on one area that appeals to you.

Free-write about why this category appeals to you. It can be just one sentence, or maybe you end up writing a full page. Don't judge what you write; just let your thoughts flow directly onto the page. You won't show anyone this. It's just for you.

For example, maybe mental self-care appeals to you because you love puzzles. Write about the first time you remember enjoying a puzzle as a child. Maybe social self-care appeals to you because you feel disconnected from your friends. Write about what those relationships mean to you. Maybe physical self-care appeals to you because you miss hiking. Write about what your body feels like before, during and after a hike.

LIST OF SELF-CARE IDEAS & ACTIVITIES

I n this chapter, you'll find a huge list of self-care activities to get the wheels turning in your brain. Of course, this is not an exhaustive list. You can be creative and come up with your own self-care activities.

Sometimes when we are stressed, just the idea of having to decide what to do overwhelms us. You should have a go-to self-care activities list to take the stress out of having to decide and brainstorm. Just taking the first step is often the hardest part, but once we sit down to write, or put on our running shoes, the rest just flows from there.

So, this list is to help you take that first step. Some of these activities could fall into multiples categories at once, or into different categories based on how you approach them. For example, a hike in nature could be emotional, spiritual, sensory or physical. I've just included each activity once and separated them as best as I can, but know that the categories are not rigid.

Also, some activities may be things you can accomplish in just a few minutes (spend time in the sun), while others are lasting activities that become a regular routine (join a new club.)

ACTIVITY

For this chapter, I'll let you know a bit about the activity before we start. Get a scrap piece of paper (or open a note on your phone) and write down the self-care activities that immediately jump out to you as something you'd like to do.

EMOTIONAL SELF-CARE ACTIVITIES

- Journaling
- Crying
- Laughing
- See a therapist
- Declutter: clean a room or just one drawer
- Help someone with a small act of kindness
- Ask for help from someone else
- Unplug from your devices for an hour
- Play! Be goofy or silly
- Make a list of compliments people have given you in the past, or reach out and ask for new ones

SENSORY SELF-CARE ACTIVITIES

- Listen to music
- Sing along to music
- Eat a favorite food
- Snuggle up under a soft blanket

- Meditate
- Light a candle
- Pet an animal
- Take a warm bath
- Walk barefoot outside or lay in the grass (grounding)
- Spend time in nature
- Take photographs
- Get fresh air
- Spend time in the sun
- Take deep breaths

PHYSICAL SELF-CARE ACTIVITIES

- Yoga
- Stretching
- Dancing
- Hiking
- Going for a walk
- Going for a run
- Getting a massage
- Taking a nap
- Playing a team sport
- Swimming
- Painting your nails, doing a face mask or get a haircut

SPIRITUAL SELF-CARE ACTIVITIES

- Attend a religious service
- Visit a religious monument or building
- Pray
- Meditate
- Read poetry or spiritual texts
- Just sit still and be for 10 minutes

SOCIAL SELF-CARE ACTIVITIES

- Call a good friend
- Write a letter to someone
- Attend a party or social gathering
- Message a friend
- Re-connect with someone you haven't spoken to in a while
- Join a club of some kind
- Join a support group of some kind
- Put an end to a relationship that is toxic

MENTAL SELF-CARE ACTIVITIES

- Do a crossword or sudoku
- Do a jigsaw puzzle
- Read a book
- Listen to a podcast or radio show
- Visit the library
- Take up a new skill or hobby
- Take a class in an area that interests you

- Read about a topic you've never learned about before
- Drive somewhere new or take a new route home from work
- Do a craft project
- Do something that takes you out of your comfort zone

ACTIVITY

OK, now that you have a list written down of activities that appeal to you, this chapter activity should be easy! Or at least, the first part is: pick ONE, yes, ONE activity from the list in this chapter.

Here's the hard part: schedule it into your calendar in the next week. Yes, you can find the time!

Here's the even harder part: when the day comes around for your self-care activity, you're NOT ALLOWED to cancel or reschedule it. Pretend this is an important meeting with your boss. No, wait, pretend it's your boss's boss. Or your favorite celebrity. Whatever works for you! But pretend this is with someone *so* important that you simply *cannot* not do it, no matter an earthquake, a traffic jam, a sickness, or, well, the feeling that you just don't want to do it.

Remember: this meeting, after all, *is* with the most important person you shouldn't cancel on: yourself.

THE BENEFITS OF SELF-CARE

In this chapter, I'm going to tell you why we are setting out on this self-care journey together. You've found your way to this book, so you already have an interest in what self-care can do for you. But I think the benefits are even more profound than you may think.

Self-care all comes back to our view of our own self-worth. Often, we say we're not taking care of ourselves because we're too busy or stressed or have other obligations. These are just surface-level reasons. The true reason we are not finding time for self-care is because, deep-down, we feel we don't deserve it.

When we start to take care of ourselves more seriously, we start to love ourselves more. Just by caring for ourselves, we can boost our own self-esteem. Beliefs come from actions, not the other way around. You don't need to believe you are worth a spa day to make it happen. But once you make it happen, you begin to believe it.

Another example: maybe you don't believe meditating for 15 minutes every day will have any benefits to your life. That's fine. Do it anyway, if it's your chosen self-care activity.

When you start to meditate for 15 minutes every day, you'll start to have a calmer mind, a more present and focused awareness, and a less reactive emotional balance in your life. Then you start to believe that meditation can bring benefits to your belief.

They say seeing is believing, but I say *doing is believing.*

So, when you start to care for yourself with the self-care activities and routines listed in this book, you start to raise your own self-esteem. When you start to care for your body as if it is precious (and isn't it? Without it, you'd be...nothing!), you start to believe that it is. Maybe you don't feel a lot of love toward your body now, but when you start to treat your body nicely, you begin to believe it is worthy and beautiful.

This is an especially short chapter because the activity in it is very important, so I want you to have plenty of time to explore it.

ACTIVITY

Think of an important relationship in your life, someone who loves you. Think of how that person treats you. Most likely with kindness, compassion, forgiveness. Think of the love that person feels for you. Think about how it makes you feel to receive that love. How does it make you feel to know that this person is always there for you? How do you feel in response to this person, in knowing how they feel about you?

Either think about these topics, or do some free-writing on them for as long as you wish. Have a specific person in mind, and be as specific as you can. Was there a specific thing they did for you that was kind? Something they said to you that sticks in your mind? Either an affirmation of their love, of your relationship, or a compliment?

Now, for the next part of this exercise, I want you to write about yourself in the same way. Maybe you don't feel very kind to yourself at the moment, or you don't feel a lot of self-love. That's OK. Write about what is possible. How would you feel if you felt true love from yourself? Would it feel similar to the love you feel from that other person you wrote about in the first part of this exercise?

What could you achieve in your life that you've been hiding from or putting off because you aren't kind enough to yourself or can't forgive yourself?

Think of the benefits of having a relationship with yourself that is as deep and loving as that of a friend, romantic partner or family member. Go as deep as you can with this activity to see the most benefit.

SELF-CARE IS A HABIT

In this chapter, I'm going to focus on incorporating self-care into your daily life.

Self-care would be easy if it just meant that every time we felt like we needed a break, we could schedule a week holiday and treat ourselves with an all-inclusive resort. Unfortunately, that's rarely the reality because of our over-packed schedules, our commitments, our budgets, and what actually makes us feel good.

You can't take a sabbatical from your life whenever you feel like you need some me-time. You have to incorporate self-care into your life. You have to make the space each and every day—yes, everyday!—to give yourself more compassion.

On a daily basis we often rush through life, going from task to task, and we forget to check in with ourselves. If we leave our decompression until we get home at the end of the day, we're already stressed and exhausted. A much better method is to decompress throughout the day instead of just at the end.

For example, just checking in with how you are feeling is

one of the easiest and best forms of self-care you can do—just being aware of yourself and being present. Fortunately, this is a form of self-care that is easy to incorporate into your daily routine.

Set a reminder on your phone for once or twice throughout the day. When this reminder comes up, no matter what you are doing, you can take five deep breaths. Feel your feet on the floor and the sensory experience of the room. Identify how you are feeling physically, emotionally and mentally in that moment. Sometimes just naming how we are feeling helps us gain some distance from it.

Or maybe you build a self-care habit. Maybe you spend the last five minutes of lunch journaling, or you wake up 15 minutes earlier to be the first one up and enjoy your coffee as you look out the window—not racing to get ready or looking at your phone, but just sitting in silence and appreciating.

Another way to incorporate self-care into your daily routine is to make it a habit or take up a recurring activity. Maybe you've always wanted to learn how to knit or to roller skate. Join a local club, class or team and then stick to the schedule. It will be something you look forward to all week, and therefore something that has lasting benefits outside of just the hour you have to practice per week.

Self-care should be activities that you want to do. They are mini-indulgences. Often, we spend so much of our lives doing what we feel we should do, or what we feel we have to do. Self-care activities are those that you want to do. They don't need to have a purpose; they can be silly or random or "pointless." The whole point is to do something just for you.

Be aware as well that sometimes self-care activities, if they are new hobbies or passions, can become just another thing you have to do. Let's say you take up roller skating at the local rink, and then you join the roller dance team, and then you have another obligation. Try to remember why it is you started your self-care activity, instead of making it just another item on your to-do list for the day.

Building self-care as a habit is the important part. On good days when you are feeling great and energized and motivated, doing a small self-care activity will be easy. It's the days when you are feeling stressed, busy and tired that making the effort for self-care will be hard. So, this is the most important time to do self-care. Remember, self-care doesn't have to be huge: it can be taking a 20-minute rest, watching a funny video on YouTube, or just taking five deep breaths.

But when you make self-care into a habit, you make it a part of your life, and that's the important part. Self-care is daily, not a once-in-a-blue-moon treat.

Treat yourself every day; you deserve it.

ACTIVITY

Pick a self-care activity that takes less than five minutes to do. Over the next week, try to do this activity every day. They say it takes 21 days to build a habit, so aiming for three weeks is even better. But for now, start small.

SELF-CARE IS A LIFESTYLE

Self-care is not only a daily habit, but a lifestyle. What do I mean by lifestyle? I mean the overarching way you live your life.

Sometimes we let healthy ways of life slip. When we have a family that needs taking care of, or a big project at work that needs all our focus, we forget to pay any attention to how we are living our lives. How much sleep are you getting? How often are you eating foods that fuel your body and mind in healthy ways? How often are you getting outside? Or doing a little exercise? Are you taking care of your mental health?

In popular culture, the idea of self-care might mean tucking in for four hours of Netflix with a big tub of ice cream. While a bit of indulgent self-care can be OK sometimes, real and lasting self-care is the kind that really makes you feel good, inside and out.

Netflix and ice cream is a temporary fix. It's like a Band-Aid. Sometimes we do have just a little cut, and the Band-Aid will help. But sometimes, our wrist is sprained or our arm is broken, and a Band-Aid just won't do.

So, self-care is a healthy lifestyle. True self-care means doing things for yourself that help you feel better for longer than the activity lasts. Self-care has lasting mental, physical, emotional, spiritual and social benefits. They are activities that truly feed your soul, not just your surface cravings.

Eating healthy and getting some exercise may be the last things you want to do to take care of yourself when you're feeling down, but these are the activities that will make you feel good for hours and days afterward. This contrasts with the TV and ice cream, which will make you feel good in the moment, but may make you feel guilty, bloated and regretful once they end.

When you are evaluating self-care activities, ask yourself how long the benefits will last. Is this an activity that will make you feel good while it's happening, but even worse afterwards? Or is it something that will nourish you in a deep and lasting way?

So, evaluate activities: is this chocolate a tiny indulgence that I will appreciate? Or a double-serving that will make me sick? Is this friend someone who supports me, or someone who always tends to bring me down? Yes, even in social settings, we can have people in our lives that aren't good for us, but we continue the relationships for whatever reason. Don't let any activity go without scrutiny.

Overall, self-care is about being kind to yourself. And being kind to yourself in the long-term sometimes means kicking your own butt into gear to get off the couch and go for a walk, breathing that fresh air and seeing some sunshine, even if you don't want to in the moment. In a way, self-care sometimes means being a bit tough with yourself.

Often, we're in a place where we're in dire need of self-care because we've let our immediate indulgences, cravings, and knee-jerk emotional reactions get the best of us. Self-care doesn't mean giving in to these. It means taking the time to figure out what really makes you happy and feel cared for in a lasting way.

This is not always easy to figure out, but with this book, it is a journey that is worth going on, and one we'll help you with.

Getting Unplugged

Now I want to mention an aspect of self-care that may be left out of many discussions of the topic.

In this day and age, I want you to pay special attention to self-care in relation to digital devices and being 'connected' all the time. Being connected to the world, the news, work, friends and messages 24 hours a day, seven days a week is enough to leave anyone drained, morose and overwhelmed.

While connection can be self-care in itself, not all connection is good. And it is easy to be over-connected in our current society. Let's take a minute to focus on how unplugging on a daily basis or taking sabbaticals from our devices can be a form of self-care.

When we think of a healthy lifestyle, we think of exercising and eating right. But one very important form of health is getting away from screens and devices. Connecting with nature, with ourselves and with our bodies is so important for feeling grounded, present and healthy.

Though it may be hard at first to put down your phone, tablet or take a break from the TV, doing so will ultimately help you connect with yourself.

Easy ways to go without your devices is to take a walk without your phone, or eat a meal without your phone nearby. Allow yourself to be bored. Allow your mind and thoughts to wander. Being bored is healthy for us. We don't need constant stimulation. Remember that unplugging—just for 20 minutes or for an entire weekend—can be a self-care activity.

ACTIVITY

Look at the habit self-care activity you chose in the last chapter, and the self-care activity you chose from the list of activities chapter. Evaluate these activities. Do they make you feel good in the short-term, medium-term, or long-term? Are they nourishing and healthy, or indulgent? If they are not the best lifestyle self-care activities, is there a way to make them healthier? If not, consider swapping out for a healthier self-care activity.

SELF-CARE IS KNOWING YOURSELF

Self-care is all about YOU. And that means knowing yourself. How can we care for ourselves if we don't know ourselves? It may seem like knowing yourself would be something you wouldn't even have to think about. After all, you spend every waking moment with yourself. How would you not know yourself best?

But often, our ideas about who we are or what we truly like are skewed. They're influenced by who we want to be or wish we were, our society and culture, our family and friends, our work environment, and our pasts. Each of us is complicated and full of contradictions. We may love meeting up with friends one night, and the next night, relish our time alone. Sometimes alone time makes us feel lonely. Sometimes social activities make us feel lonely. We can have one persona in one situation, and act differently in another. Who we are is constantly evolving, but are we in tune with these subtle shifts?

If you've chosen a self-care activity of joining a recreational softball team again because you loved it when you played 10 years ago, will you still love it? Maybe you will reconnect with a sport that you truly found joy in back then, and you'll still love it now. But maybe you've grown into someone who doesn't really get enjoyment out of softball anymore, and that's OK, too. Our interests and passions change, and sticking to one idea of ourselves is not good for our self-care.

The more you know about yourself, the better you'll be at administering self-care. For example, a lot of people would look at massages as a form of self-care. Personally, I find them a bit boring and awkward. So, if I was trying to force myself to get massages to relax, it's actually doing the opposite and stressing me out. I'd be much better off spending that money and time on something I actually enjoy, instead of something I feel I'm supposed to enjoy. Maybe a computer programming course, which would be a mental form of self-care.

Paying attention to what you actually like and makes you feel good is important in self-care. You're the only one you need to please here. Don't worry about whether you're doing self-care "right" or the "correct" way. The most correct way is getting the most out of it that you can.

A form of self-care is spending time getting to know yourself. Noticing what gives you energy and makes you excited versus what drains you is essential to understanding yourself.

Personality tests are one way that you can learn more about yourself. You can often find free assessments online to help you learn about your personality. Some of the most famous personality tests are:

- Enneagram
- Myers-Briggs

- StrengthsFinder

THERE ARE LOTS MORE. What matters isn't that you pick the right test, but what you decide to find meaning in with the results. If the test tells you that you would love analytical forms of work like math and spreadsheets, but you know you love writing, you have the ultimate say. Don't follow what the personality test says as the law.

The tests are just a means to get you to be more self-reflective. Maybe you have never considered yourself an analytical person before, but now that you think about it, maybe you *are*. Maybe more math-focused work would benefit you. The personality test results are a catalyst for thinking about yourself in new ways.

Read the descriptions of the personality type the results give you, and see what sticks out to you. Taking the time to get to know ourselves and who we truly are is one of the best forms of self-care.

ACTIVITY

TAKE one of the personality tests listed (or find another one you want to try). Read the results and see if you've learned anything new about yourself. How can you apply something you've learned to your self-care activities?

SELF-CARE IS NOT SELFISH

Now that we're this far into our discussion of self-care, I think it's time to point out something very important: self-care is NOT selfish.

People make excuses for not taking care of themselves that sound very altruistic and legitimate. "I have too many family obligations." "I have too many work obligations." "Other people need me too much."

While all these things may be true, you can't take care of someone else before you take care of yourself. By replenishing your own stores of energy and self-love, you are then free to give your energy and love to others.

Self-care can sound indulgent. Why would you spend all that money and time on yourself, when there are other more practical uses for them? But self-care is about allowing yourself to play, to feel freer, to feel more in control of yourself and of your life.

Even if you set aside just $5 a month as your "play money" for self-care, you can spend it on something truly enjoyable. A new set of colored pencils for your adult coloring books. Your favorite chocolate bar. A train ticket to a place near your town that you've never been. The point is that you give yourself license to do something that doesn't have a point or practical purpose, but is just for fun, for play, and for YOU.

Sometimes we believe that we are not deserving of our own love and nurturing. This can be one of the most difficult realities to face in your self-care journey: finding the underlying reason why you're not taking care of yourself. Maybe someone said something hurtful to you when you were young, and you've believed that you're inferior ever since.

Maybe you've had toxic relationships in your life that have left you with low self-confidence. These are harsh roads to explore, but if you do, you'll be healing wounds that only you can heal. If you feel truly overwhelmed and lost, see a mental health professional. Otherwise, do journaling or find books that help you resolve past issues and experiences that are affecting your own view of your self-worth today.

You deserve to enjoy your life.

You deserve kindness, from others and from yourself.

You are worth love.

You are worth compassion, from yourself and from others.

You are worth self-care.

A Self-Care Note for Parents & Caregivers

Here's a very important note about self-care in our current culture. These days there's something online called "Mommy Shaming." This ridiculous practice involves criticizing the way other parents raise their children, usually on a Facebook post or other social media post.

I'm here to say that you shouldn't be afraid of mommy shaming on your self-care journey. Whether you are a parent, grandparent, caregiver or guardian, you have the right to still be your own person. You are in charge of someone else, it's true, but that doesn't mean you stop existing.

Taking time for yourself or doing something that other people might think is selfish does not mean it is. You are the own judge of your life, and an adult. You have the power to assess what you think is right, what you need and what your family needs. As a leader in your family, you need to nurture yourself and your relationships to be able to lead properly.

ACTIVITY

Journal for 5-10 minutes about what you believe you deserve. Then write down what you believe a good friend deserves.

Afterward, read back what you have written. Do you have any limiting beliefs about what you think you deserve? Did you notice you were much kinder to your friend than to yourself? We are usually kinder to others than to ourselves, which, when you think about it, just doesn't make sense. We are our own best friends and should treat ourselves as kindly as we treat others.

SELF-CARE STARTS IN YOUR BRAIN

I have written a related book to this one called *Self Talk*, and it is all about how we talk to ourselves in our brain. This is an essential topic to discuss for self-care as well. Even if we go through the motions of being kind to ourselves by joining the local gym, visiting the local spa or catching up with a good friend, we can still be cruel to ourselves with our thought patterns. In this chapter, we'll discuss how to change your negative self-talk to positive self-talk.

We are constantly running unconscious patterns of thought in our heads. And they really are patterns that get stuck in there, like the refrain to a catchy song. They are unconscious, meaning we don't realize we're doing this. We don't realize how harmful it is. They say the average person's inner mental chatter is about 80 percent negative. But the good news is that each of us has the power to change our inner mental chatter. It is as simple as rewiring the patterns and creating new ones. It may not be easy, and it will take some work and time, but it is very much worth it, and your self-care journey will suffer without this important aspect.

Let's discuss a few different types of negative self-talk.

THE FIRST TYPE IS FILTERING, which is when we filter out the 10 compliments we received about our new haircut and focus on the one person who didn't seem like they liked it very much. Why not focus on the compliments instead? Our brain is wired to lean toward the negative. Be aware of this.

The second type is **catastrophizing**, which is when we go down a thought spiral of negative thinking. When one bad thing happens, we assume more is to follow, or we think of all the bad things going on in our life. Realize that one bad thought leads to another, and try to stop a negative thought spiral.

The next type of negative self-talk is **personalizing**, which is when we assume that bad things that happen are directed specifically at us, instead of realizing that bad things happen all the time, and we shouldn't take them as personal attacks.

Polarizing is when we see things as black and white, good and bad, with no room for considering the silver lining, the blessing in disguise, or that most things in life are gray, neither good nor bad but somewhere in-between. It's up to us which side we focus on.

Rehashing is dwelling on the past and getting caught up in what we should have done or should have said. Be kind to yourself by forgiving yourself for things you feel you've done wrong in the past. Dwelling on them doesn't help and only makes you feel bad about yourself. See what you can learn to do differently next time and move on.

Rehearsing is worrying about the future. You may imagine all the negative ways your work presentation can go, trying to prepare for each one. Instead, focus on how your presentation will go right, and take some of the stress off of yourself.

And finally, the last type of negative self-talk is **blaming,** which is when we take on other peoples' problems or bad days and find a way to make them our fault. Everyone is responsible for their own reactions and dispositions. Don't blame yourself for someone else's problems. Caring about another person is different than blaming yourself.

NOW THAT WE'VE covered a few types of negative self-talk, you'll be more aware of how you use these types in your own head. Just being able to recognize a type of negative self-talk helps you get some distance from it. Remember that you are not your thoughts. You have the power to change them.

Now let's look at some strategies for changing your negative self-talk into positive, self-caring thoughts.

1. **Recognize your inner critic.** One way to get some distance from the critical voice in your head is to give it a name. Yes, an actual name. See your negative thoughts as coming from another person, not from within yourself. What would you do if someone in real life was as mean to yourself as you are in your head? You'd hopefully ignore them and realize they are trying to hurt you. So, imagine your negative thoughts are coming from a different person, and dismiss them.

2. **Investigate your thoughts.** Another strategy is to investigate a negative thought when it comes into your head. Ask yourself, where did this thought first come from? Was it something a teacher or parent said to you when you were

little? Something you read? Can you identify this thought as one of the seven types of negative self-talk? Ask yourself, is this thought useful? What might a more useful thought be? A more positive thought on this topic? When we question our negative thoughts about ourselves, we realize they often have no basis in reality. Your negative thoughts are guilty of being useless, mean and unfounded in reality until proven innocent. I think you'll find they are usually guilty of all of these traits!

3. Use affirmations. It's hard to replace a repetitive negative script when we don't have anything to replace it with. Write down nice things about yourself. If you have trouble, ask friends for compliments, or what your strengths are, or what they admire about you or like best about you. Write down the nice things you'd tell a friend, and then change them from "you" to "I".

ACTIVITY

What's something you say to yourself on a regular basis that is not very nice? Investigate this thought, and find a positive thought with which to replace it.

CONCLUSION

Thank you for reading this book on self-care. I hope you have come away from it with at least one change you can make in your life, which will help you to be kinder to yourself and to take better care of your most important relationship.

I hope this book will become a reference for you as you go through your self-care journey. Its short length makes it an easy book to revisit when you are feeling down or stressed. I didn't want to pack this book with lots of fluff, because I believe taking action is more important than hearing the same advice over and over.

The most important part of this book moving forward is that you do take action. If you haven't done any of the end-of-chapter activities yet, go back through the book and pick out one to do in the next day. You may feel resistant to taking action, but the first step is often the hardest. Once you get the ball rolling, you will find that the self-care, self-love and self-compassion you can give will snowball. Each action you take, however small or big, builds on the last, and it will keep building and building.

You will feel greater self-confidence, greater presence and awareness in your daily life, and feel more in tune and appreciative of your body.

I have one more end-of-chapter **activity** for you:

Of course, making these changes is not easy. Is there someone in your life you are close enough with to tell them you are embarking on this self-care journey? It might feel scary to open up, but try telling one person what you are trying to accomplish, and ask for their support. Ask them to check in with you later this week and ask if you did the self-care tasks you set out to do.

You will be surprised how supportive this other person will be. Maybe they will even be intrigued by your journey and want to go on it with you. Though self-care is ultimately up to you, having another person going on their own journey, side by side, will help keep both of you accountable.

I am so happy I am able to share the strategies in this book with you, and I truly hope you found them helpful. As an indie author, I depend a lot on reviews for my books, so if you have one minute and something nice to say, please leave me a review. [insert link]

I can also be reached at aston@walnutpub.com if you'd like to reach out individually. Readers of my previous books, *Small Talk*, *Self Talk* and *Minimalist Living,* have reached out to say the books have changed their lives in small and large ways. This is why I write, for you, my reader.

My books don't connect with everyone, but that's OK. If this book didn't connect with you, I hope you still took away one practical thing. I believe self-care is something we all need more of in our life. Developing the most important relationship in your life—with yourself—is so important for a healthy and happy life, one in which we can give our best selves to other people.

Always remember:

> You deserve love and compassion.
> You are worth kindness.
> You are a good person.
> **You deserve loving, gentle self-care.**

Your Author,

> Aston Sanderson

PART III

SMALL TALK

HOW TO TALK TO PEOPLE, IMPROVE
YOUR CHARISMA, SOCIAL SKILLS,
CONVERSATION STARTERS & LESSEN
SOCIAL ANXIETY

HOW TO TALK TO PEOPLE, START CONVERSATIONS,
IMPROVE YOUR CHARISMA, SOCIAL SKILLS
AND LESSEN SOCIAL ANXIETY

SMALL TALK

By Aston Sanderson

INTRODUCTION

T hank you for taking the time to download this book. You've taken the first step toward becoming an interesting conversationalist and someone that new people you meet will remember.

Why Small Talk Matters

Meeting new people can be hard for anyone, but with these proven strategies and tips, you'll find yourself growing more confident and beginning to enjoy the challenge of meeting someone new and developing a real, personal connection with them.

In these chapters, you'll learn how to increase your social skills and lessen your social anxiety. We will take you through techniques of good listening, provide a list of conversation starters, address body language, and more.

At the completion of this guide, you will have all the tools you need to get out and meet new people immediately with greater ease and confidence.

Once again, thanks for downloading this small talk guide. I hope you find it to be helpful.

Why Is Small Talk Important?

Humans are, in our very essence, social animals.

We seek approval from others, and feel most comfortable fitting in with our families, our peers, our culture, and the world at large.

Being socially inept can mean being rejected, which evolution has taught us is a bad feeling we'd like to avoid. Societies have been based for thousands of years on people getting along, working together, building community, and marching together toward progress.

"Wow—all that, just from talking about the weather?" is what you might be thinking.

But it's true! We're social animals, and talking is our way of getting to know one another. Small talk is a way for people to break down barriers and show one other through conversation that the situation and the person they are talking to is safe. Only after establishing the tiniest bit of trust can we begin to form actual relationships through deeper conversation with those we don't know. Everyone you have met, except, perhaps, for your family members, once started as an acquaintance you most likely had to engage in small talk.

We've all done it, but no matter how much experience we have, meeting a stranger can be hard for anyone. But you don't need to hide away from fear of feeling nervous or having social anxiety.

Even for the most experienced, gregarious conversationalists, meeting new people always comes with the risk of rejection.

In these chapters, you will learn how to conquer your fear, master your body language, find good topics to talk about, and finally get out there and start meeting people with confidence.

One More Note

Just one more quick note before we get started—reviews can make or break an indie author's career. If you enjoy this book, I'll ask you at the end to leave a short review, as it's one of the biggest things you can do to support me if this book helped you in any way.

I love to get feedback from my readers, and I read every review personally. I thank you for your time. Now let's get started!

MINDSET & APPROACH

Like anything in life, the most important thing about small talk is the way you approach it.

All the strategies, tips, hacks and conversation starters won't make a difference if you're stuck in a negative pattern of thinking. Don't get stuck in a fixed mindset based in fear, self-doubt, or irrationality.

What is a fixed mindset? A fixed mindset means you think that who you are at this moment is who you have always been and who you will always be.

You may think:

- *"I'm not good at meeting new people."*
- *"I always say the wrong thing and make a bad first impression."*
- *"Social skills are just not my thing."*
- *"I'm happy just staying home; they won't miss me at the party."*

But those are all fixed mindset phrases.

You should focus on a growth mindset. A growth mindset means that you realize and accept that things are constantly changing in your life, all around you, and in your skills and actions.

You may not be the best conversationalist today, but everyone can acquire some strategies (like you've done by buying this book), practice them, and become better over time.

So let's turn those fixed mindset phrases into growth mindset phrases:

- *"I'm not good at meeting new people"* becomes *"I'm getting better at meeting new people."*
- *"I always say the wrong thing and make a bad first impression"* becomes *"I am learning what to say around people and improving the first impressions I make."*
- *"Social skills are just not my thing"* becomes *"Social skills are an area of my life I have the capacity, ability, and desire to improve upon."*
- *"I'm happy just staying home; they won't miss me at the party"* becomes *"I am discovering new things about myself by getting out of my comfort zone, and I may be surprised how much fun I can have at a party."*

See how the "I am only this way" type of thoughts become "I am becoming better and constantly improving and working on it" thoughts?

So, even if you think you are not the most beautiful social butterfly out there, you can remember that (to use a well-worn metaphor) all butterflies were once caterpillars.

If you believe that you are bad at social situations, you have already sabotaged yourself.

Believe that you can get better, and you've already taken the first, and possibly most difficult, step.

In the next chapter, we'll look at how you can address your nerves and calm them.

NERVES & HOW TO CALM THEM

We cross the threshold into the party. We deliver the wine we brought, hug the host, smile, and excitedly catch up with her.

But then—the host has dozens of other guests to attend to. She disappears as the doorbell rings.

Now what do we do?

The party seems full of people who are frightening to approach—people who *may* not like us. It's certainly a possibility.

We imagine walking up to someone and starting a conversation, but we also wonder, will they like us? What will they think of us? Facing rejection is tough, no matter how small it is. Even if someone we don't know at all rejects us, we wonder why, and may get down on ourselves.

Facing all that overthinking, when a party is just supposed to be fun, can be hard!

So how can we overcome nerves?

Breathe

It sounds simple, but when we are nervous, our bodies can take over without us realizing it. We may start to sweat, our breathing becomes rapid and shallow, our thoughts race, and our stomach can feel upset.

But what causes this physical reaction? Just our thoughts. So it works in reverse, too. Calming our bodies can also help to calm our minds, just as our minds affect our bodies. This is called the mind-body connection, and it has more influence than you think.

So re-enter your body when you are feeling nervous in a social situation. Become aware that you are just standing in a room with people, not on the savannah about to be eaten by a lion, like your body's nerves are conditioned to respond to through evolution. You are safe. Remember to breathe.

Focus on your breath, and your body will calm. Your heart rate will slow, your breathing will be more even, your stomach will settle, and your thoughts may stop racing.

If you can, count to five while breathing slowly in through your nose, filling your stomach, not your lungs. Feel the deep breath fully. Then, release the breath to the count of five as well, through your mouth. These deep breaths will calm your nervous system.

If you're at a party, do these breaths under the radar. Take the opportunity to practice your breathing in the car before you go into the party, or while you are walking down the block. You can ask to use the bathroom straightaway and then do some deep breathing in there. Don't be the weirdo standing in the corner, huffing and puffing!

Remember That Your Reaction is Normal

Public speaking is many people's no. 1 fear, as it's so ingrained in our biology. As comedian Jerry Seinfeld said,

"According to most studies, people's number one fear is public speaking. Number two is death. Death is number two. Does that sound right? This means to the average person, if you go to a funeral, you're better off in the casket than doing the eulogy."

And even the most practiced public speakers still get nervous before going on stage, often experiencing the bodily symptoms we just discussed in the last section. Even if they don't feel nervous in their mind, people's physical reactions tend to be similar.

No matter how confident you are, you can still feel nervous.

So remember that you are not the only person at the party, or the meeting, or work event who is feeling nervous.

If you remember this, you won't feel so alone. It's okay to admit to yourself that you are scared. Just remember that a lot of other people are too.

In fact, getting a bit of distance from our emotions and reactions can allow us to the space we need to acknowledge them, while also lessening their power over us. This is a technique from meditation called "labeling." When you label a feeling or emotion, it has less power over you, because you recognize that you are not the emotion; you are just experiencing the emotion, and it is temporary. So when you're feeling stressed, think to yourself:

- I am feeling stress.
- I acknowledge that I am having thoughts of nervousness.

- My body is reacting to this situation with nervousness.

Even just the simple act of naming your emotions and feelings can allow you some relief from them.

Meet A Lot of New People

Another way to calm your nerves is to practice!

In psychology, when someone is afraid of spiders, a tactic used to help them get over that fear is called "systematic desensitization."

This means exposing the person over and over to spiders. First, it may just be progressive photos of spider, from small to large. In the next step, the psychologist will hold a spider at a distance. Finally, the patient may be able, by him or herself, to hold the spider, having conquered the fear slowly, through these increased stages.

You can use systematic desensitization in your life as well, for meeting new people.

If you get used to meeting new people all the time, you will slowly become less frightened of it, just like the person with a fear of spiders. You can start slowly, by just making it your goal to make small talk with someone you already know, perhaps a coworker at the office whom you don't talk to much. Next, move on to a bigger goal, like making extra small talk with your coffee barista in the morning, or someone familiar, but who you don't really know.

Then move on to making small talk with a stranger to you, but maybe someone that a friend of yours knows. If you always get brunch with your friend Lucy on Sundays, ask Lucy to bring along a friend of hers you've never met before. There will not be as much social pressure, as Lucy will be there to facilitate conversation, but you also get the opportunity to practice small talk with a complete stranger, in more of a safe environment.

Keep increasing your goals each week, slowly, and soon enough you will find yourself feeling more confident in meeting new people.

Remember that at first, meeting new people will feel difficult and scary. But with each subsequent social situation, you will feel more and more comfortable.

Social Anxiety

We all suffer from some form of mild social anxiety. It is nerve-wracking to approach a stranger and face the fear of rejection. We also fear awkward silences, or that someone might be mean or rude to us.

But often, we are "catastrophizing" an event or situation in our head. If we feel the slightest bit nervous about something, we can imagine all the ways it will go wrong, visualize the worst-case scenario, and convince ourselves we need to get out of that situation, pronto.

But of course, the worst rarely transpires, especially in the way we see it in our minds. We worry no one at the party will like us and we will be laughed at. We worry we will completely forget the words to our work presentation speech, or won't wear our pants to work that day, as the common nightmare goes. These mental crutches hold us back, however. Because our brains are naturally inclined to think of negatives rather than positives, we don't think of the *best-case scenario.*

But what if we did? We can imagine that we connect really well with someone at the party, perhaps someone we can see again as a friend or potential dating partner. We can imagine that our work presentation goes so well that a coworker or our boss compliments us on it afterward (and we remembered to wear our pants!)

If we don't attempt to exercise a bit of intentionality, our imagination can run wild and get away from us. So, a tactic you can use if you experience a social phobia is to imagine all the good ways a scenario can go, and try to minimize all the negative things you imagine. Or, you can make an attempt to limit your imagination entirely, and try not to think about possible outcomes for the event, presentation, or date. After all, it hasn't transpired yet, and worrying does nothing to improve the future, it only ruins the present moment, as the saying goes.

Another strategy for social phobia, when it keeps us from getting out of the house in the first place, is to remember that you only need to attend the party for a half hour. You can always leave. Sometimes, I have trouble pushing myself out of my comfort zone if the idea of an event is making me nervous, or I convince myself that I'd have more fun staying in. But I only need to remember that I can return home whenever I like, and then I know that I can push myself to go out for at least 30 minutes.

One final note about social anxiety: Though many of us probably suffer from a mild form of social shyness, if you suffer from diagnosed social anxiety, it is best to consult a trusted and licensed medical professional about steps you can take.

In the next chapter, we will discuss how *listening* is actually the most important part of *talking.*

GOOD LISTENING IS YOUR GREATEST ALLY

It may sound weird to say that the best way to improve your conversational and small talk skills is to *say nothing at all*.

But that's exactly what this chapter is about.

Often, when we are engaged in a conversation that puts us out of comfort zone, we focus so much on saying the right thing and our minds racing that we forget to ever listen to what the other person is saying.

The idea that people are terrible at listening to each other may be comforting. When you realize that a lot of people you talk to may not even be listening to what you say, what does it matter if you're not interesting? But on the other hand, what kind of world is that, if we all go around talking and talking and never listening to each other? We can all work to become better listeners and engage each other on a deeper level.

Being a good listener is *extremely hard.* But it's one of the best ways to increase your likeability and the ease with which you get along with other people.

And just like the actual talking part of the conversation, listening skills can get better with practice.

Here are three ways you can improve your listening:

Picture It

When you listen to someone else, it is easy to get wrapped up in thinking about your own experiences and how they relate. "Picture it" is a great strategy to converse with someone new, as shared experiences or having things in common is a great way to break down barriers.

But if the person begins sharing the details of their recent trip to the coast, and you immediately start imaging your most recent beach trip and thinking about what you can share about it, you are totally missing what the other person is saying.

So when the person you are conversing with talks about the sailing adventure they went on, try to follow along by imagining it in your head. Can you picture the boat they took? When they mention that it was a three-day trip, you can picture them sleeping on the boat each night. But, wait —sleeping on the boat, was that hard? You know how it feels to get motion sickness in a car.

Now you have a great follow-up question. Maybe they actually found it really peaceful to sleep on the boat, like being rocked to sleep. Maybe they kept having nightmares it was sinking. Either way, you have a very specific question that shows you were really listening. The best follow-up questions are pulled from these key details. If you instead were spacing out and thinking about your own beach trip, and then realized they were talking about sailing anyway, so maybe you shouldn't share your story about getting sunburned at the beach, then you might default to a boring, unrelated question, like, "So, what do you do for work?" It's then obvious to the other person that you weren't listening, and maybe they feel they weren't telling an interesting story, and your conversation is probably not going very well.

Instead, just listen! Really listening opens up limitless paths for your conversation, and the only way to find those paths is to really listen for the details of someone's experience.

If you can imagine their story and experience it in your mind, you will probably ask yourself the same questions that person did while experiencing it.

So use your imagination to your advantage! Keep your brain busy by focusing on picturing the other person's experiences, instead of your own personal experiences and the story you want to tell next.

Give Your Full Attention

It may sound obvious, but don't get distracted. Resist the urge to pull out your smartphone, even if it's just to look something up to share with the person, because your brain will immediately jump to thinking about all the notifications from social media or unread emails.

So remain fully engaged and present with the person you are speaking to.

Keep eye contact, and don't let your gaze wander around the party, event, or restaurant, wherever you may be. This body language signals that you are bored or looking for an out of the conversation, so remain focused. We'll talk more about body language in another chapter, but for now, just know that if you are giving your mental attention to a person, your body will show as much. It's actually easier to actually give your attention, rather than trying to fake it by appearing interested but really zoning out.

Giving someone your full attention, especially in the distractions-on-steroids world we live in with all of our gadgets and the whole of human knowledge at our fingertips, is one of the most respectful and generous things you can do. Wouldn't it be lovely for someone to just listen to you, fully and presently, without checking their email?

If you give the people you know (and those you have only just met) your full, undivided attention, you may find you start to receive the same in return more often.

Imagine You'll Tell Someone Later

One of the best tricks for comprehending something and remembering something is to imagine that you'll be explaining it to someone else later.

This is a strategy that students can use for tests, but it's also a mind frame you can use when listening to someone else speak. We recall information better when we process it in our own minds and have to repeat the information back.

If you imagine you will tell someone later about the conversation, you will be more likely to pay attention and remember the important parts.

In the next chapter, we will move on from listening to, yes, finally, the actual *talking* part of small talk!

WHAT TO SAY

Ugh, not the weather again!

Small talk gets a bad rap. Many people don't have particularly fascinating or important opinions or observations about the weather, and they don't want to hear anyone else's. They don't care about the local sports team. They don't want to talk about where they work, and for how long, again.

But remember that small talk plays an important social function in our society. This seemingly meaningless banter provides a way for us to get to know each other and is a non-threatening way for us to engage with one other. Have you ever been having a bad day and had the cashier mention that the feel-better ice cream you just bought yourself is their favorite flavor too? If so, didn't that make you smile? Connecting with others, even through such small, surface-level interactions, is extremely important to us social animals.

Even if it just makes you feel a tad better, interacting with people can help you feel not so wrapped up in your own thoughts, even if it is just "small" talk.

Small talk provides a low barrier of entry so we can all approach and talk to each other. If you walked up to strangers and asked them, "What is the most important memory from childhood?" you'd be pretty off-putting, to say the least.

But that's a question we'd feel comfortable discussing with best friends, our partners, or close family. At one time, each of those people was a stranger, too. And that wasn't the first thing we said to them.

So realize that anyone you speak to could become one of your close friends. It just doesn't happen overnight, or in the span of one conversation. Be patient, and make yourself and them comfortable at first by sticking to easy topics.

It can still be fun to talk about topics that aren't threatening or very deep.

You can try:

- *Travel*
- *The host you both know*
- *Movies or TV you find you have in common*
- *The city you live in*
- *What you're doing for a coming holiday, or what you did for one that just passed*

People love to talk about themselves, so if you can get someone to talk about themselves, instead of the weather, it will probably already be much more engaging for both of you.

Small talk doesn't have to be small! We'll show you how to have better small talk conversations, ones that actually lead to getting to know someone, in the next chapter.

But first, here are some ideas of what to say when engaged in small talk:

Find Common Ground

The first strategy for what to say in small talk is finding common ground. Any topic will be easier to discuss when both people in the conversation have something to add about it.

The most obvious and immediate thing you both have in common, unless you're talking on the phone, is your immediate surroundings. So you can comment on the immediate situation.

If you are at a party and mention the good music, or the great snack table, or how great the turnout is, and the stranger you mention it to says more than one word, they are saying it's okay to engage them in conversation. This is a great way to take something you have in common and test the conversational waters.

Maybe you both hate the current song that's playing, or maybe you both love it.

Even if it's a stranger in the elevator, maybe you both just stepped inside from the rain, and the city's weather is obviously something you have in common. You can say something like "I hope this wet pattern we've been having stops soon," or "I can't remember if my windows are open at home, have you ever done that?"

Just say something innocuous and see where it takes you.

Following from the common ground strategy, if you come across something you both have in common, more than the immediate situation or party you find yourselves at, make sure to explore that topic as much as you can! Maybe you both grew up playing soccer every summer. Maybe your grandmas are both from Southern California. Maybe you both love dogs!

It could be anything, but sharing a common quality or passion with someone new instantly endears us to them, especially if you find that you both participate in an unusual hobby, such as stamp collecting or Brazilian jiu-jitsu. We tend to get excited when we find someone who shares our particular brand of weird, whatever ours is!

Give Compliments & Information

The next strategy for what to say in small talk is to be *giving*. When you offer something to another person, the inherent value we place as a species on reciprocity means a person will want to give something back to you. Reciprocity is a pretty large concept, but for the purposes of small talk, it just means that offering something, like information about yourself, or a compliment, makes it easier for the other person to want to share something about themselves, as well.

First, let's tackle compliments.

Everyone loves receiving a compliment. Don't go overboard, but you can comment on something small and simple. Something like, "I love your shirt" is enough to get started chatting to someone new.

Of course, be aware that compliments can also easily come off as a little too weird or forward, especially as a man complimenting a woman. Don't get too personal with physical compliments, and stick to things people are wearing or carrying instead of commenting on their hair or body.

Next, let's look at giving something besides compliments: Information.

Conversing is all about sharing. If you don't share, the other person will find it more difficult to bounce back to you in the conversation if you don't give them anything to go on.

If they ask you where you went to college, instead of just saying, "Iowa," you can say, "Iowa. It was a very small town, which I loved, because I grew up in a big city."

That's revealing something meaningful about yourself—that you grew up in a city but also enjoy small-town life.

You could follow it up with, "Do you prefer the city? Have you spent any time in the country?" and now you have a conversation flowing!

Maybe the person you're talking to says (like our previous tip of commenting on the surroundings) something as small as, "Have you tried the popcorn at the snack table? It's so good."

Instead of just saying, "Yes, it's good." Or "No, I haven't," you can add, "Popcorn is basically the only reason I go to the movies. I've seen a lot of mediocre movies just to eat popcorn because movie theater popcorn is the best."

Now that person can agree or disagree with you, or ask you about a recent movie you've seen. They have a lot of options, since you've revealed something about yourself rather than just a "yes" or "no" answer.

The more you put forth, the more you should get in return. Of course, don't go on a 20-minute diatribe about your personal problems, but be willing to open up a bit, even if it feels unnatural.

Stay Positive & Light

Going off of the idea of not getting *too* personal right away, keep the conversation positive and light to begin with.

It's best not to start complaining or talking about something you don't like immediately after meeting someone new. No one likes to be around someone else who is super negative!

Also avoid the topics of health, religion, and politics, which can be personal and controversial. Even if you think someone will probably agree with you on these topics, you can never be sure, and never "judge a book by its cover." Even if someone holds the same beliefs as you, talking about these heated topics can quickly become an intense conversation, and not in a good way.

If the topic is heading toward something in one of these areas, you can try to gently steer it away.

If you're talking about (of course!) the weather, and the other person mentions the crazy storm that happened on election day, then asks you whether you went out in the storm to vote, you can steer the conversation away from its political implications and bring up a new topic. By bringing up a new topic instead of re-directing just to the weather aspect of their comment, you help avoid giving the other person an opportunity to bring up politics again.

Maybe say something like, "Oh yeah, I was out in that storm. I was worried about my dog all day! When I got home I couldn't find him, but eventually I found him hiding in the shower!"

Now you can safely talk about pets or dogs or fear of storms.

If the person is insistent about starting a political discussion, it may be best to move on. We'll give you strategies for exiting conversations in future chapters in this guide. But first, in the next chapter we'll talk about keeping conversation flowing by asking questions.

NOT ALL QUESTIONS ARE CREATED EQUAL

Questions, questions, questions!

After good listening, asking good follow-up questions is probably the most important part of mastering conversation and leveling up your small talk game.

So what makes a good question? Let's find out:

Good Questions are Open-Ended

Aim to ask questions that allow for nuanced answers, in order to encourage the other person to expand. Questions that can be answered with a simple "yes" or "no" can be a conversation killer.

Remember the question words:

- *How*
- *What*
- *Who*
- *When*
- *Where*

- *Why*

As you're getting to know someone in your conversation and feeling more comfortable, breaking out "why" is a great strategy to use to probe a bit deeper.

If someone mentions that Bucelli's is their new favorite restaurant in town, you can ask them why, and then they have a chance to share more about something they're excited about and feel very positively toward. Sometimes people are caught off-guard by "why" questions, because as we go about our lives, we rarely ask people why they think or do something. We just accept what is.

They may have to think for a minute, but then maybe they'll say something like, "Bucelli's ravioli tastes just like my grandma used to make. She actually grew up in Italy. She taught me so many bad Italian words when I was a kid."

Their grandma sounds like a fabulous cook and a spunky lady. What a great topic to ask more about!

Good Questions are Superlative

Good questions are also superlative. "Superlative" refers to the extremes of something: The best, the most, the least, the craziest, or someone's favorite.

When you ask a follow-up question, asking a superlative is a good way to have someone talk about something that they find engaging.

If someone mentions that they've been living in the same neighborhood for 10 years, you can ask them what the best thing about living there is, or their favorite thing about it. Clearly, they've stayed a while!

If someone mentions that they've worked in HR for

years, you can ask what the craziest way someone quit a job was.

If someone loves traveling to Las Vegas, what's the biggest winning they've ever witnessed at the casino? The biggest loss? (But try to make the question impersonal. For instance, "Have you ever seen someone win more than $10,000 at once, or set the slot machine off on one of those crazy ringing frenzies?")

Asking superlative questions makes for an easy way to open someone up about their most memorable experiences. Sometimes, I find that when someone asks me a superlative question, it sometimes is something I haven't thought about before. That makes that person a lot more memorable to me, as the conversational experience they provided was unique, interesting, engaging and new.

Don't Interrogate

Remember, don't let the other person do all the talking!

If you're feeling nervous, you may be inclined to share less instead of more. But then you give your conversational partner less to work with and ask you follow-up questions about.

So don't only ask questions, and don't ask a ton in rapid succession if you're not getting good responses back. This may be a sign that they're not interested in being asked so many questions about the topic you're inquiring about.

So also share about yourself for a bit, and feel comfortable doing it. If someone is sharing details about themselves with you, you should do the same as a courtesy with them.

Conversation is like a tennis match or a game of catch: You hit the ball back and forth, and each person should be contributing about equally. If someone is talking at you, this won't be a pleasant conversation experience, like getting tennis balls repeatedly hit at you when you're not even holding a racquet, or getting a ball thrown at you without a mitt. In the next chapter, we'll give you tips for exiting such conversations.

FEEDBACK & ENDING A
CONVERSATION

Being good at small talk is not only about knowing how to talk and listen well. It's also about knowing how to end small talk conversations.

Sometimes, it's just the natural end to a good conversation and meeting someone new. However, sometimes we meet someone we'd rather not spend time conversing with (someone who brings up controversial topics, talks *at* us instead of to us, or in some way makes us uncomfortable). Don't feel badly about leaving conversations like this. You know the difference between a conversation that's not great because, though the people have good intentions, they're just not good at casual talk, and a conversation that's uncomfortable because one person is just a blowhard or jerk.

In this chapter, we'll look at how to end conversations gracefully, whether you can tell your conversation partner wants to leave, or you would like to end a conversation.

Signaling the End of a Conversation

First, let's look at how to notice if your conversation partner is using coded social cues to exit a conversation. They may try to let you know in a subtle way, as most people do when engaged in small talk.

Before we look at that, though, don't feel bad when someone is finished having a conversation with you. You're not going to be the new best friend and Most Interesting Person everyone has ever met, and that's true for everyone at all times.

Having a fabulous connection with someone the first time you meet them is rare, and you should appreciate it when it happens. But in a lot of cases, friendships or even acquaintances are built up over time through repeated meeting, shared experience, and many conversations, not just one or two.

Someone leaving a conversation doesn't mean that it was bad. Maybe the other person is in a hurry or needs to speak to someone else at the work function to ensure they get that promotion they were hoping for. Maybe they want to catch up with someone they haven't seen in months who is also at the party. You don't know the reason someone is done talking to you, but often, the reason is not that you are not worth talking to.

Here are some cues to look for that someone is ready to end a conversation:

- *They're not making eye contact, but are instead constantly looking around*
- *They say "It was nice to meet you" or "It was nice talking to you."*

- *Their body language is "closed." This could be crossed arms, or their body pointing away from you and the conversation*

You can also use any of these tactics on your own to exit a conversation.

How to Leave a Conversation

It's also nice to give someone else an out of a conversation. If you have only been talking to that person for a long time at an event with a lot of people, you both should meet more than just one person. You can say something like:

- *"Well, I'm sure you have a lot of other people to catch up with."*
- *"It's been so great talking to you, but I'm going to mingle a bit"*
- *"It's been great to talk to you, but I think I should meet a few of our host's other friends, too."*

If you need to be a bit more forceful (like with that jerk blowhard), you can use "I need" statements. It is in our psychology to respect the things people say they "need," even if it's just a "want" in reality. You can say things like:

- *"Excuse me, I need to use the bathroom."*
- *"I need to refill my drink. It was nice talking to you."*
- *"I need to make a phone call, excuse me."*

Like all things in life, even good conversations must come to an end. Don't feel bad about it, as that just means it's time to practice small talk with someone new. In the next chapter, we will discuss some phrases you can use as conversation starters when you meet new people.

CONVERSATION STARTERS

At a loss for topics to talk about, ways to approach someone, or how to keep the conversation going after it's stalled a bit? In this chapter, we'll add on a few tips for starting conversations and provide a list of good questions to spark interesting discussion.

Tip: Remember Names

It is incredibly important to remember people's names.

Many books about winning friends or getting people to like you suggest using a person's name as often as possible when talking to them. However, this "trick" has been around as advice for about 80 years, and it has been given as advice in the realm of sales. So I actually would advise against this strategy. We're so used to salespeople and telemarketers doing this that it tends to feel very salesy, off-putting, and fake.

However, I highly recommend remembering someone's name and using it once or twice in the conversation, usually at least when you say, "Well, it was nice talking to you, Jen," and leave a conversation.

When we meet someone new, we're getting so much sensory input and are so wrapped up in how we're coming across that the opportunity to actually hear and remember a person's name sometimes slips right by us. We worry about our handshake and grip (or whether we'll shake hands at all, as in some informal settings it's no longer customary), how we'll introduce ourselves, what the person looks like, what we look like, how much eye contact to make, and on and on.

How often have you met someone and realized less than five seconds later that you have absolutely no idea what his or her name is? What you can do in such a situation is be more mindful when you're meeting a new person, and really focus on their name, instead of all the other sensory stuff we get wrapped up in.

If you still forget their name, you can politely ask something like, "By the way, I'm so bad at names, I'm sorry, but what is your name again?"

They'll probably be flattered that you even ask, as most people just try to avoid the topic of names once the initial introduction is over!

Prepare Beforehand

Another tip for beginning conversations is to prepare beforehand, if you know you're going into a situation where small talk will be made.

On your drive over to a barbecue, think of at least two or three conversation starters to bring up if a conversation begins to stall.

Scan a newspaper before you leave the house to see if

there's a big news story you can talk about. (Though, once again, avoid politics, religion, or controversy.) Think of what movies recently came out and whether you have any interesting information about them, like reviews or awards, even if you haven't seen them.

When there is silence in a conversation, you may immediately assume it's an "awkward silence." Do not have this mindset, however.

A period of silence will always feel much longer than it actually is, so don't feel stressed about how long the break in conversation is.

Also, the silence is just that: A break. Think of it as a transition in the conversation to a new topic. Perhaps you have naturally exhausted the things both of you have to say about the current topic, and you can now move on to something new. Or, perhaps you feel the conversation is finished and this is a good time to use one of your exit strategies from the last chapter.

Let's move on to a list of conversation starters you can use.

A List of Conversation Starters

Use the questions below to keep a conversation flowing once it has stalled or slowed, or to begin a new conversation.

- *Have you always done this [profession], or have you worked as anything else?*
- *If you could fly anywhere in the world at no cost tomorrow, where would you go?*
- *What was the best job you had growing up?*
- *What's the best advice you've ever gotten?*

- *What's the strangest compliment someone has given to you?*
- *Do you have a book, movie, or TV show that you love, but everyone else hates? What about something everyone else loves, but you hate?*
- *If you could only eat one food for the rest of your life, what would you choose?*
- *Does your family have any recipes that have been passed down for generations, or that are secret?*
- *What was the last travel experience you had?*
- *What's your favorite thing to do on the weekends?*
- *Have you ever lived anywhere else? How was this place different?*
- *Do you have a hidden talent, or a surprising hobby?*
- *What's your favorite app on your phone?*
- *Have you read any good books recently?*
- *Have you ever had a boss who asked you to do something crazy?*
- *What's your favorite little-known restaurant?*
- *If you could have any superpower, what would it be?*
- *What would you teach a college course on, if you could?*
- *If you could have any animal as a pet, what would you choose?*

BODY LANGUAGE

We say a lot with our bodies, and we read a lot about how other people are feeling based on their body language and facial expressions, even if we don't realize we're all constantly communicating with this secret language.

So you need to make sure that your body language is saying what you want it to. Your body will probably naturally show how you're feeling, so if you're interested in speaking to someone, you will show it.

However, if you're not really interested in speaking to someone, or you're feeling nervous, your body may be sending the wrong signals to the other person.

In this chapter, you'll learn how to read someone else's body language.

Your Body Language

When you're trying to communicate friendly body language, your body should generally be "open." That means no crossed arms, crossed legs if you're sitting, or turning your body angled away from the person you are talking to.

Other body language tips are:

- *Smile and appear friendly*
- *Make eye contact, but don't stare*
- *Stand a comfortable distance away from someone, not too close.*
- *Sit at comfortable distance, not too close for awkwardness, not too far to hear*
- *Avoid using your phone during the conversation*
- *Avoid excessively touching your face or hair or other nervous habits like picking at your nails or fidgeting*
- *Don't tap your foot, as it could appear that you are impatient to leave the conversation*
- *Don't chew gum*
- *Relax your shoulders*
- *Don't hold your drink or anything in front of your chest, as this can communicate that you feel guarded*

It's also helpful to mimic the body language of the other person. Obviously not in the way we did this as kids to annoy our siblings ("Mom! She's copying me!") but this is a natural tactic we use unconsciously when we're getting along well with someone. If you become more aware of your body, you may notice yourself doing this unconsciously.

For example, you both may be nodding, or leaning in slightly, or moving your hands in the same way, or holding your drinks the same way.

Don't, however, overdo body language. In general, refraining from large movements or small tics will make the conversation and what you are communicating with your body flow more smoothly.

Above all else, a friendly, genuine smile can usually be worth more than any undesirable body language you may be displaying. So remember to relax and smile!

Reading Body Language

When you're speaking to another person, pay attention to their facial expressions, and this will communicate a lot that the person may not be expressing directly through their words.

Also be aware of how the other person is standing, and their posture and the way they hold their head.

For example, building on the tips we gave you in the last section, be aware if someone else is putting off these body signals. They could just be nervous, but they may also be communicating that they're not that into the discussion you're having.

Here are a few things to keep in mind when reading body language:

- *A genuine smile will create wrinkles or creases next to the eyes; fake smiles involve the lips only.*
- *If someone is mimicking your body language, it means they like you and the conversation is going well.*
- *Someone may be lying if they hold eye contact for an extended period of time.*
- *Raised eyebrows or pursed lips can mean that the person is experiencing discomfort.*
- *A tight jaw means the person is stressed out.*
- *Crossed arms or legs are "closed" body positions that may mean the person is not that open to your ideas or the conversation.*

- *An excessive amount of head nodding may mean the person is worried about getting your approval.*
- *Notice where the person's feet and legs are pointing. If it is away from you, they may be signaling they want to escape the conversation.*
- *Excessive blinking or facial movements can indicate anxiety.*
- *If someone looks at the floor a lot, they are probably shy or embarrassed.*
- *Normal eye contact is meeting the eyes and holding eye contact about 80% of the time, and usually not for more than seven seconds.*
- *Leaning in towards you means the person is interested in the conversation (or maybe that the party is very loud!)*

The last point that should be made about body language is that it can vary a bit from person to person, so don't automatically give up on a conversation if someone is crossing their arms, or think you have a new best friend if someone is leaning into the conversation. Use body language cues in tandem with other context and what you know about small talk to assess how things are going.

That's just a brief intro to body language, as we could spend books explaining all its finer points. In the next chapter, we'll look at small talk for dating. If you're in a committed relationship already or don't have an interest in dating, you may find this chapter interesting and helpful in the general sense of turning small talk into deeper talk.

SMALL TALK FOR DATING OR: TURNING SMALL TALK INTO DEEP TALK

When we start with small talk, we often want to make the conversation go a little deeper. Some people really hate talking about the weather (I'm not one of them; I find it endlessly fascinating), or some people hate talking about their job. No matter your feelings about small talk, the ability to turn a small talk conversation into something more, whether that's on a date or just making a new friend, is the key to lasting connections with people.

In this chapter, we'll look at a few ways to turn small talk conversations into deeper-level conversations.

Stories Are Better Than Facts

If your date conversation gets stuck in small talk, you may never find out if you really like the person and want to see him or her again. You want to get to a deeper level of talk and figure out if this relationship could work out.

The thing, is you don't need to put a lot of pressure on the first date to figure out if they want kids, want to settle down in the same city, or are in debt. Those things can wait!

For the first few dates, just try to assess if you enjoy each other's company and conversation.

Still, you don't want to talk about the local sports team the whole time. So some of the strategies we talked about in this book to use at a meeting, conference, or party can be deepened and expanded upon to make "small talk" into "deep talk."

First, let's talk about storytelling. Storytelling is extremely important to humans, and it is what we find most engaging in a conversation, instead of a straight exchange of facts.

So on your date, don't just exchange facts, but be more interesting by telling stories.

For example, as a response to the question, "What do you do?" you can offer a story or detail, instead of only your job title and company name. Instead of saying "I'm a fourth-grade teacher," you can say, "I'm a fourth-grade teacher, and one of my favorite parts of my job is seeing kids figure out new things and get excited about them. I had a girl who said she'd never painted before our art lesson last week, and now she's bringing me paintings she's doing at home."

That's a great short story that opens the window to talking about something you're passionate about—seeing kids discover new passions—while avoiding the boring parts of your job, like how much you hate grading or the long hours.

Storytelling is immediately more engaging than a simple statement of fact.

Here are a few engaging first date questions to ask:

- *What's a big influence in your life right now?*
- *Who has been your best teacher or professor in your life?*

- *What should I know about you that I may not think to ask about?*
- *What would your ideal Saturday look like?*
- *What makes you laugh a lot?*
- *What's your biggest goal you're working toward right now?*
- *What's the worst thing about dating?*
- *Any pet peeves I should know about?*
- *What were you like as a child?*
- *What's your favorite place in the entire world?*

And one last tip: Doing something engaging for a date, like a cooking class or a hike, will bring you closer together than grabbing a drink or eating a meal. There will be less silence to fill, and you'll have the experience to talk about as well to get to know each other. This may help the conversation flow more easily.

Stay Open-Minded

One of the way humans make sense of the world is by putting things into boxes, labels, and categories. If we couldn't do this, the world would be frighteningly complex (even more so than it is already!) We have pigeons, eagles, parrots, and crows, but we know these are all types of birds, so they go in the bird category. This is helpful for us to understand what to expect when we encounter a bird we haven't seen before.

Sometimes, though, these labels are too simple, and they can keep us from discovering new things or being open-minded. This is especially true in dating, when we're trying to assess whether this stranger is the kind of person we like and want to hang out with, the kind of person we could possibly fall in love with, the kind of person we're attracted to or not, or the kind of person who could end up hurting us.

That's a lot to figure out and a lot of pressure, and sometimes it can make us feel vulnerable. So we try to answer these questions quickly, with irrelevant identifiers like what color hair someone has, what they do for work, where they're from, etc.

If everyone we've met from California has been kind of a jerk, and we learn our date grew up in California, it's a shorthand mental strategy to put them in your Cali-jerk box and label. If they're a corporate lawyer or a professional musician, we have boxes and labels for those people as well. But all these boxes just serve to keep us from possibly really connecting with someone we haven't imagined ourselves connecting with before.

How does this relate to the small talk on your date? Try to collect more information about passions and what's important to a person than what they do for a living, where they went to school, or another question that might be a "box" question.

Instead of asking someone what they do for a living, ask them, "What's your favorite part of your daily routine?" or "What do you care about at the moment?"

These questions leave a lot of room for the other person to go very deep with their answers, or stay a bit more surface-level but still engage in a way they might not have if you just asked about work.

It's only by going a bit deeper than our boxes, though it can be uncomfortable, that we can truly get to know someone, and not just their label.

Online Dating & Chat

A chapter about small talk in dating would be incomplete in this day and age without acknowledgment of how much of our small talk happens in chat.

No matter what kind of dating website or app you're using, there's bound to be a little bit of text chat before meeting up in person. I do recommend, however, that you move the chatting offline as soon as possible. There is so much we can learn about a person through a live meeting that we absolutely cannot know from text chat. When we talk in person, we have the added context of body language, voice inflection and tone, facial expressions, and immediate conversation, versus text responses that can be mulled over for the perfect witty response for hours.

And you may feel turned off by the way someone text chats, but everyone has a different approach to the unwritten etiquette rules of messaging online. So don't judge someone by the *way* they chat (judging them by the content of their chat is okay, if they're rude, etc.) Just accept that you don't really know what someone is like until you meet in person. Some people are just bad at texting and may come off as robotic when they don't intend to.

But when you're involved in text chat, it's best to use the same principles that apply to in-person small talk.

Use the person's name, and ask them about something they have mentioned in their profile or on linked social media accounts. Did they just attend a concert you heard was really amazing? Did they say they love animals? Did they recently go on an exotic trip?

Asking something other than "How are you?" or "What's up?" shows that you care enough to take a few minutes to learn something about a person instead of using a formulaic response. You may be surprised how many people don't take this simple step, and how much genuine niceness can stand out in online dating.

Small talk, once again, is the way we judge whether or not someone is "safe" to talk to, and unfortunately, can be a barrier to entry to deeper conversations. That doesn't mean it has to be boring, though! Use the techniques from this book, and you'll find yourself easily segueing from small talk to more interesting and revealing conversations, whether that's in your dating life or another area.

In the next chapter, we'll talk about recovering from social faux pas.

WHY YOU'LL MAKE A MISTAKE AND
WHY IT DOESN'T MATTER

In this chapter, we'll make one last note about small talk, now that you're becoming an expert! So here goes:

None of us are perfect. Even the greatest communicators, most gregarious people, and biggest and most beautifully-winged social butterflies stumble sometimes in a social situation. Maybe your conversation partner isn't making it easy for you and you have to do all the work. Maybe you had a bad day at the office and your mind is still at work. Maybe you're just having an off day or misjudged a joke that you thought would be funny. That's all totally okay!

We all make mistakes, and rest assured that everyone thinks about themselves a lot more than they ever think about you. Try to think of your most embarrassing moment from grade school or middle school. You can remember it pretty vividly, can't you? Did it happen in front of a lot of people? How many of your classmates do you think remember it today? Can you think of other people's embarrassing moments you witnessed in school? Probably not as many as you can think of for yourself.

So remember to relax. It will all be okay! It feels overwhelming and terrible in the moment, but no one will remember your embarrassing social faux pas.

Another thing to remember about social skills is that they are learned. No one is born a social communicator. We all have to grow up and learn language and the ways people interact in our specific culture. If being gregarious and popular were innate, people would be revered across cultures. But it can be hard to talk to someone who doesn't share the same social rules and conversation markers from another country.

Some people are predisposed to liking social interaction more, or have had more experience or are more naturally inclined to it. But these are just social clues that can be learned, so you can learn them too. Everyone thinks they're worse at small talk than they actually are.

Your social skills are a muscle, and just like when you are weight training, you need to stretch them, work them, and keep stretching and working them and challenging them to grow those muscles. Right now, you may feel like you're lifting very little socially, with our weight-lifting metaphor. Maybe you can only lift the bar. But with practice, you'll be able to add a bit more weight, and then a bit more.

Weight training has a strategy of "training to failure," which means lifting until your body physically cannot do it anymore. Your body "fails" at the task. So each time you make a social faux pas, you're training your social skills to overcome failure, and therefore getting stronger.

After you go through these strategies and start to learn more about social skills, you will definitely make some missteps. And once again, that's totally okay! It just means you're improving. As long as you learn from the situation, realize what you could have done better, and then move on, you're doing wonderfully.

Your social skills and small talk muscles are growing with each interaction, especially those that you feel you didn't totally crush. Don't freak out and go into a downward spiral thinking that you're bad at small talk. You are growing, little caterpillar and future social butterfly, and that's what important.

In the last chapter of our small book on small talk, we'll summarize the important points we learned about socializing.

CONCLUSION

It's time to use what you have learned in this small talk guide. I hope that you've gained strategies you can use right now to improve your social skills and lessen social anxiety.

Remember, you can get out there today and use what you've learned. Remember these general tips:

- *Be confident and have a growth mindset*
- *Accept that you will feel nervous and know that it's normal*
- *Use the surroundings to start conversations*
- *Ask open-ended questions*
- *Share about yourself; don't give short answers*
- *Have friendly and open body language*
- *Avoid controversial topics*
- *Let the other person politely end the conversation or do it yourself*
- *Remember that when you feel you made a social flub, it means you're working your conversation muscles and are getting better!*

I have one more thing to ask you.

As an indie author, reviews can be the lifeblood of my books. If you felt you received at least one good tip you'll use from this book, I ask you to please share your positive feedback with other readers by leaving a review.

I personally read every review, and really appreciate hearing from you, my all-important readers. You're the reason I write books. I want to help you grow. I appreciate you.

Sincerely,

Aston

PART IV

MINIMALIST LIVING

DECLUTTER YOUR HOME, SCHEDULE &
DIGITAL LIFE FOR SIMPLE LIVING (AND
DISCOVER WHY LESS IS MORE)

minimalist living

Declutter your home, schedule & digital life for simple living (and discover why less is more)

ASTON SANDERSON
2nd Edition: Updated & Expanded

INTRODUCTION

Welcome to "Minimalist Living." The basic principle of this book is: You have too much stuff. And it's not making you happy. In fact, I'd wager that all your extra stuff is making you decidedly unhappy.

But there's a way out from underneath that pile of stuff that's weighing you down and holding you back.

We'll discuss the underlying reasons that you, me, your friends, your coworkers, strangers on the street — all of us — are so compelled to buy, and why we clutter our lives in the first place.

We'll use economics and philosophy principles to look at consumerism and minimalism.

We'll discuss your custom minimalism plan, and why a minimalist lifestyle doesn't match what you've probably seen it portrayed as in the media: It doesn't mean living with bare, white walls, one lamp, one chair and owning just two outfits.

You'll learn how to win back your sanity, time, money and freedom to live a life that is not minimal, but that is abundant in your values and what matters to you.

We will save your life from your stuff.
Are you ready?

WHAT IS MINIMALISM?

To understand minimalism, I'm going to ask you to start with a simple question. The question is:

Have you ever packed for a vacation or trip?

If your answer is yes, then you have already practiced minimalism.

Minimalism can feel very inaccessible and unreasonable to those who have only heard about it from news articles. You've probably wondered if minimalism is really for you, if you have the strength to narrow down your possessions, or if you would be the same person without all your things. These questions are normal, and a misunderstanding of what minimalism can be has made it seem inaccessible to many people. But there's a reason minimalism was brought on your radar, and a reason you are reading this book right now. You want to see if it is for you.

And as we learned with my vacation packing question, you have already tried minimalism. And guess what? You're still alive!

Minimalism is *en vogue* at the moment, and that means

that every decluttering guru, minimalist blogger and minimalist author (who convinces you to get rid of all your
things but at the same time, buy their book for your coffee
table) has a guaranteed method to make you finally happy.
You can be just like the extreme minimalism guru once you
follow their plan. Once you get rid of all of your clothes,
your home and your devices, you too can live in a van, own
three shirts, two pairs of pants and one pair of shoes, and
grow your own vegetables out on the open plains.

OK, maybe I am exaggerating a bit. But many minimalists live in barren, cold apartments with barely any possessions. They say this makes them truly happy.

But my form of minimalism is different. My minimalism
is for everyone, not just extremists. And I am going to do
something very radical with my minimalism book: I am not
going to promise I can make you happy.

Crazy, right?

But you have come to the point where you are looking at
minimalism as a lifestyle because you've acquired an overwhelming amount of stuff and you've realized that it doesn't
make you happy. Things aren't going to make you happy.
But guess what? The *absence* of things isn't going to make
you happy either.

So, if you follow the advice in this book, what can it give
you? Paring down your possessions — we'll talk home,
clothes, schedule and time commitments, digital clutter and
more — gives you the space and room, free from distraction,
to explore what does make you happy. I can't promise you
happiness, but I can promise that you're taking the first step
toward it by making the space for happiness in your life.

When you pare down what isn't essential in your life,
you make the room to discover what is essential. Often,

what is essential and happiness-making is doing fulfilling work, investing in meaningful relationships with the people in our lives, and focusing on improving our physical and mental health over improving our "status" as displayed by our possessions, apartment and flashy car.

But we'll talk about that more in future chapters. For now, let's get back to that travel metaphor.

No matter whether you are a light packer or a heavy-duty packer who prepares for every possibility, just by packing for a vacation, you have practiced paring down your things. So even if you packed three large suitcases for a weekend beach getaway, you still practiced whittling down your possessions from a house- or apartment-full to just three suitcases. How did you decide what was essential? If you were going to a warm, beach climate, you probable brought at least a swimsuit, suntan lotion, and a good book. You probably left at home your fall jacket, your desktop computer, and the other 100 books on your book shelf.

You spent a week by the shore, and you didn't need all those things you left at home. In fact, many people, when their luggage gets lost on their holiday, find that they enjoy their vacation more once they buy some random clothes and accept that they just can't have the things they intended to bring. You will find that embracing minimalism can feel freeing in the same way. At first, getting rid of things and adapting to a new philosophy and way of life will be uncomfortable and scary, and you may feel compelled to turn back. But once you relax, open yourself up to the experience, and allow the benefits of minimalism into your life, you will be pleasantly surprised.

Now that you've had a brief introduction to this rene-gade style of minimalism, and have breathed a sigh of relief that I'm not going to try to convince you to live in a small, barren and white apartment, we can begin to start diving deeper into the psychology of consumerism and minimalism.

In the next chapter, we'll examine the different reasons we humans love to collect so much stuff in the first place.

WHY WE CLUTTER OUR LIVES

People collect possessions and knick knacks for so many reasons. In this chapter, we'll look at a few reasons that we get so buried in our lives under all that clutter and stuff.

The first reason that people buy excessively is that they are trying to fill a void. I know I have experienced this, and I'm sure you have, too. That void may be many things: Perhaps it is a particularly hurtful breakup in a relationship, perhaps it is the loss of a relative, perhaps the loss of a job, a dissatisfaction with work, or any other feeling of inadequacy or lack. When someone tries to fill a void with shopping, they can never patch the hurt, not permanently. A person will try to distract themselves from feelings of worthlessness or grief by putting a temporary patch of retail therapy over the wound. But the rush that shopping provides does not last or sustain us in any meaningful way.

The dopamine rush of purchasing something new actually ends the second we buy the item (or shortly after unboxing it, if you enjoy unboxing). Psychology shows that people actually get more of a dopamine rush (the chemicals that create feelings of pleasure in our brains) from anticipating a purchase than actually making it. Once you buy something, it becomes just another old thing you own that you are unhappy with. It may not happen right away, but I bet it happens more quickly than you think that the things you own become dusty, gray, old and boring in your eyes. Think about it: Everything you own now was once a new item to you. Some things may have been hand-me-downs, but many things you own were probably purchased new. You probably anticipated buying the item before you went to the store, maybe you spent hours or days researching online the different options available to you, you agonized over making the right purchase, and then you felt excited on purchase day. Handing over your hard-earned money for the item was satisfying, but once you got it, you were a bit disappointed to see you weren't significantly happier than before you owned the item, at least on a consistent daily basis. And now, you barely think about that item or your much-anticipated purchase. You may even be thinking about upgrading to a different model, different color, better quality, or just newer version. What was once so craved by you now leaves a bad taste in your mouth. And so the rapid consumption cycle goes.

So if you are shopping and acquiring things to fill a void within yourself, you need to recognize this feeling. We'll talk more about dealing with this feeling later, but first, let's identify another reason you may be shopping and buying things.

Another reason that we as humans buy excessively, as opposed to filling a void, is to attain an ideal. This is called aspirational living. Basically, it's the idea of trying to live your life like an Instagram celebrity or a model in a magazine. You want to buy a lamp or end table to "finally complete the look of the living room," or buy a pair of earrings or a new dress to have "the perfect thing to wear for the weekend party." But it's hard to actually attain these goals: The Instagram pictures are filtered and photoshopped, the homes in the magazines don't exist and no one lives in them.

Let's look at two ways aspirational living hurts us. When we look for perfection outside ourselves, we can never fully grasp it. If you try to satisfy a feeling you have inside of you by having a nice living room, or a great outfit, that thing is not you. It's another thing you own. It exists outside of you. You can only find true happiness from within yourself. Another way this assumption about attaining perfection is harmful is that perfection is never an attainable goal, or at least it isn't one that leaves us satisfied. Perfection is hard to maintain. Those who strive for it in any area of life will find themselves struggling to be happy with anything, even something that is 95% "perfect." They can only look at how something lacks, or what it is missing, instead of appreciating what is. There are so many wonderful things in life, but a perfectionist can only focus on what's missing from the picture. Living your life this way is a guarantee to live unhappily.

Those are the two main reasons we acquire stuff: We either want to stave off feelings of lack, or we crave a feeling of fullness. No matter which end of the spectrum drives us, neither are healthy reasons to spend the money you work your whole life to earn just to acquire things you have to take care of.

In the next chapter, we will look at how you can stop living a life driven by these feelings, and how you can live a life of abundance, and what that means.

LIVING A LIFE OF ABUNDANCE

Minimalism may sound like the opposite of abundance. Abundance means a very large quantity of something. So you could say most people are already living lives of abundance: They have so many possessions cluttering up their lives, they are basically swimming in abundance! But in this chapter, we are going to explore a new definition of abundance.

People often think that minimalism means living with almost no possessions in a barren home. But minimalism is just a sliding scale and spectrum, and an optional path to happiness. Maybe you want to reject the idea of minimalism. If you do, that is your choice. But first, ask yourself: Are you possessions, and your goals to acquire more and nicer possessions with each passing year, really making you happy? If not, it's imperative that you re-assess your relationship to the things you own. This is all minimalism is inviting you to do. You can decide how many of your possessions you want to keep, which of them to keep, and why. I will not direct you to get rid of all of your spatulas, DVDs, or old high school year books. As long as you take the basics of minimalism as you learn them here, and use them to re-assess your priorities, and you live by your priorities, then you have succeeded in minimalism.

So living a life of abundance doesn't mean owning many things; what it actually means is living a life that is abundant in the areas that are important to you.

The hard part is figuring out what is important to you. And then once you've figured that out, you must invest in those areas. The ideas in this book aren't easy, and they aren't quick-fixes. But they are changes that are possible to make, and the results you see can be incredible.

So, on to the hard questions: What are some areas you can choose to invest in, some aspects of your life in which you'd like to experience abundance? For many people, family is important. Another area that many people find important is meaningful work that contributes to society. While some people pursue this at their 9-to-5 job that they get paid for, others pursue meaningful work by volunteering or by investing in an artistic passion. Another area some people find great to invest in is their own physical body and health. People accomplish this by spending time being active by going on hikes, playing a team sport, or going to the gym while nourishing their body with healthy food and regular sleep.

While these are just general examples, refocusing your energy, time and money into these areas of your life can have so many lasting benefits that far outweigh the short, addictive highs of shopping and acquiring. Establishing meaningful relationships with friends or family is a basic human need, and has long-lasting effects on our mental and physical health. Being a part of a community is important. Pursuing meaningful work makes us feel needed on this Earth, and like we have bettered the world around us.

Taking care of our body leads to better mental fitness as well. Exercising releases endorphins, and being of sound physical mind and body means calmer, healthier approach to every aspect of our life. Physical health is often referred to as a "cornerstone" habit. Once you put more exercise or a better diet into your life, you will start to find that it leads to the formation of other healthy habits and benefits in all areas of life.

OK, are you asking yourself: Why all this blathering on about family, work and health? Isn't this a book about minimalism? You caught me! But the point of this chapter is to convince you that minimalism doesn't mean throwing away, getting rid, reducing, and cutting out until there is almost nothing left in your life.

Minimalism is cutting away the inessential, to make more room for the essential.

Minimalism is about minimal waste of time, energy, resources and money and maximum gain from time, energy, resources and money. Minimalists strive to live lives of abundance. It's just that usually, the abundance they collect and invest in isn't something you can see. It isn't a perfectly hip and well-decorated apartment, or the most chic wardrobe. Instead, it is investment in intangibles, but the things that are most likely to bring us true and lasting happiness.

Now that you understand what we're going for with living a life of abundance, in the next chapter, we'll talk about the 80/20 rule, another guiding principle of minimalism that may be new to you.

THE 80/20 RULE

The 80/20 Rule (also known as the 80/20 Principle or the Pareto Principle) is the general idea that 80% of the effects of something come from just 20% of the causes. The rule can be a bit hard to grasp at first, but once you get it, it can change your life.

The principle was developed by an Italian economist, Vilifredo Pareto, who first published his principle in a paper in 1896. He noticed the principle in many areas of his life, from big to small. He noticed that 80% of the land in Italy was owned by roughly 20% of the Italian population. He also noticed that in his backyard garden, 20% of the pea pods produced 80% of the peas. From a huge swath of land as big as a country, to the smallest pea in a garden, Pareto realized that the 80/20 rule was everywhere around us.

The 80/20 rule will apply to your life in small and huge ways, as well. The principle is often referenced in business circles. For instance, 80% of sales usually come from 20% of customers. In addition, 80% of complaints usually come from 20% of customers (and the most difficult-to-please customers are usually not the same customers who are producing 80% of the income).

How does this economics law relate to minimalism?

The applications of this rule are never-ending. Once you start looking for areas where the 80/20 rule applies, you will see them everywhere. You are probably using 20% of your kitchen utensils 80% of the time. You are probably wearing 20% of your clothes 80% of the time. You are probably accomplishing 80% of your best work (whether it's at your job, tidying your home, catching up on emails, etc.) in 20% of your time.

Following the Pareto Principle, you could probably pare down about 80% of your possessions and time-wasting and have that much more time and money to devote to intentional living, or living a life of abundance.

In terms of time, instead of spending five hours trying to complete a work task, and bouncing around between Facebook, emails, Instagram, reading four different articles, talking to your coworker, going to the bathroom, going to grab a snack, writing your grocery list and checking Facebook again, you could probably laser-focus your attention on your task, forcing yourself to complete it in 30-minute chunks, in less than two hours. We'll bring in another economics law here to explain this. Have you heard of Parkinson's Law? Parkinson's Law states, "Work expands so as to fill the time available for its completion." Often, we are trying to waste time at work because we have to clock in from 9 to 5. But if you kept track of how long each of your tasks take, you may find that there is much room for minimizing the time you spend on tasks.

While minimalism is often thought of as re-organizing your closet, it is a philosophy that can be applied to any area of life, especially with managing your time. If you are trying to create more abundance in your life by paring down your possessions, you won't feel like your life is very different if you're still spending 2 hours a day on Facebook and 4 hours in front of Netflix. So when you go through paring down your possessions, your schedule and your digital devices, remember the 80/20 rule. What are you getting the most from? What are you getting little, if anything from? Keep only the 20% that gives you 80% of the results.

Though I mentioned that most people think minimalism is just re-organizing your closet, going through your possessions is still a very important part of the philosophy. (I know you wanted to get out of cleaning out your closet, or basement, or attic, or wherever it is that gives you a headache just thinking about it. But don't worry, I'll guide you through it in later chapters). For now, we'll move onto the next chapter, where we will discuss how living a life of minimalism will save you time and money.

HOW TO SAVE TIME & MONEY

M inimalism can save you both time and money when it comes to possessions.

American society is a consumption-driven culture. Everyone is out to sell you something, and if someone promises that they aren't selling you something, they're lying to you. That's a common saying and a quite cynical view of modern society, but the U.S. is a world power because of its powerful consumption and capitalism.

A well-thought-out critique of global political and economics systems is beyond the scope of this book (and the background of this author), but suffice it to say that if you live in America (or many other developed nations in the world), you probably own too much stuff.

Have you ever thought about the booming self-storage industry, begetting entertaining but horrifying shows like "Storage Wars?" While storage is a necessity in life for people moving houses, going traveling for an extended period of time, or helping family downsize or relocate, self-storage is often not temporary for Americans. We don't only use storage when we're in-between life stages, we use it as a permanent solution to the stuff falling out of our closets and taking over the den.

We have to move into bigger apartments, buy bigger houses, or buy even more complicated storage methods for our closets and pantries to use every available inch of space, from floor to ceiling.

Getting rid of some of this stuff clogging up your life can make you feel like a huge weight has been lifted off your shoulders. Taking care of our things takes up a lot of our time, and can deplete our bank accounts as well, when we have to pay for maintenance, storage, cleaning, care and repair. If you've ever moved from one apartment to another, or even worse, from one house to another, you know the overwhelming feeling of, "How did I ever acquire all this stuff?" When we move, all of our possession are pulled out in front of us, and we can finally see all that we own. Sometimes the result can be quite shocking.

So we have to enlist friends, or hire movers, or rent a truck, just to cart our things from one place to another. If you only pared down to the essentials, you would be confident that any resources you spent moving them from one location to another, storing them, or otherwise spending extra time and money on them was a good investment, because they were things you used often, cared about, and enjoyed. But too many of our possessions are things we don't care about, things we rarely if ever use, and items that we don't actually need or want.

Not buying all these objects in the first place is, of course, the best way to save money. But we'll address that in the next chapter. We'll also address how to go through your items methodically to decide what you would like to keep later on. But for now, let's look at how getting rid of the things you already own can save you money.

The first way to make money from your things is to sell them second-hand. While some of your possessions are used, they may be in quite good working order. Electronics can often sell well on the second-hand market, as well as quality clothing. But you may find, like many people, that many of the things you have are not even opened or ever used! A quick way to make some cash from your old things that you don't want anymore is to hold a garage sale or yard sale. Even if you only make a few bucks off of each person who stops by to browse, the money adds up over several days and across many possessions.

If you find yourself something of an entrepreneur, you can also take to the online second-hand market. You can resell used items on eBay and Amazon, though some effort must be put into creating the descriptions, taking and uploading attractive photos, and then shipping your item to whoever purchases it. Once you learn the ropes of these sites, however, they are surprisingly simple and easy to sell on, and a great way to make a small side income from things you are already own that are just gathering dust around the house. Even putting in a few hours a week can produce quite a bit of extra cash, and it can be fun to watch the auction bidding.

Another way to sell your items is to go to your local thrift store or pawn shop. While many second-hand stores also take donations, some will purchase high-quality items.

The last way to make money is to donate all the things you don't want to your local charity, Good Will or Salvation Army-type store. While the donation is free, you will get a receipt from your donation and can deduct the perceived worth of your items from your next year's taxes. But be aware that how much you think your items are worth is usually much higher than their actual value! So estimate low amounts on your taxes as a safe bet.

So, now you understand how having fewer possessions will save you time in the care for them, and save (or maybe even make!) you money when you get rid of them. In the next chapter, we will look at the toughest part of minimalism: How to want what you already have.

HOW TO WANT WHAT YOU ALREADY HAVE

One of the hardest things in minimalism is truly wanting what you already have.

Feelings of contentment go against human nature by its very design. Intrinsically, in our very basic needs, we always crave what we don't have. It is like the saying, "The grass is always greener on the other side." If you can't decide between two shirts, and you buy the blue one, the gray one is sure to seem better in hindsight. But if you buy the gray one, the blue one suddenly seems the better choice. While this is an over-simplified example, I bet you can think of five items off the top of your head at this moment that you'd like to have or are considering purchasing soon.

Advertising and media can have a lot of influence over us. Actors and actresses in movies are beautiful and skinny, women in makeup commercials have flawless skin and professional athletes have perfectly sculpted bodies. Perfection seems to be all around us, constantly. If only we could look better, have nicer things, or not make mistakes, we, too, could be perfectly happy, and desire nothing else in our lives.

When we look at a beauty product, electronic gadget or new item that we crave, we envision ourselves living in the fantasy world created by advertising. Every area of our life would improve. If we lose 10 pounds, we will no longer get angry in a traffic jam. If we have the new iPhone, we'll suddenly also acquire the perfect romantic partner to take Instagram pictures with. If we have a flashy car, we'll be the type of person who vacations in the Greek isles.

We all get lost in these daydreams to some extent. Maybe you don't identify with believing your entire life will change because of acquiring a possession, but there's a deep-seated, emotional need for you craving it. Why else do you want a new dress, or a new shirt, or a new hat or pair of shoes? Unless you literally don't have any other shoes to wear, or clothes to adorn your body, you crave this thing because of some material reason. Many people all over the world own much less than the average American. They may only have two outfits and one pair of shoes, and yet, they survive. So packing our closets full (and feeling like we have "nothing to wear" when we look at dozens of outfits in our closet) is an irrational need. These irrational needs are making us unhappy.

I ask you to take a few minutes to truly think about and question your thought patterns when you decide that you need the latest tech device or new clothes or accessories. Do you really "need" it, or do you just "want" it? Unless you look deeper within yourself for the reason you are buying things, no amount of decluttering of your home will stop you from filling it back up. You need to look at the true root cause of your consumerism. Maybe you impulsively buy because you are putting off a big creative project, like writing a book, starting a blog, or getting back into painting. Maybe you are dissatisfied with the way you look, but instead of addressing the health of the body under the clothes, you keep purchasing new clothes, thinking you'll finally find the outfit that makes you feel good in your skin. Maybe you are worried or unfulfilled in a relationship in your life, and you buy to fill that need. Whatever the reason is for filling your life with more things, you need to take stock of it.

Figuring out just why you are buying things is the first step to stopping the flow of new things coming into your life. But the second step is actually appreciating the things you already have. How can you do this?

Negative Visualization

One method, as borrowed from the ancient philosophy of stoicism, is called "negative visualization." What negative visualization means is that you imagine losing the things you have, and what your life would be like without them. Sure, your raincoat feels a bit worn, as you've had it for a few years, and you'd really love to get an expensive, new and stylish rain coat. But let's imagine that you no longer want to buy the new one, because you've identified the real reason you are using retail therapy. So now you are just left a bit unhappy with your current coat. But with negative visualization, you imagine losing that coat. What if you have to leave the house, and now you have no rain coat? You suddenly appreciate how it kept you dry, how it was so easy to grab on your way out the door, how it never let you down in four years of owning it. Now when you step outside in the rain, you'll feel more appreciative of your raincoat.

You can use negative visualization for anything in your life. Maybe you have an old phone, and would really like the latest model. But imagine you had no phone at all. How would you find map directions on-the-go, or message friends and loved ones, or take photos of good times to remember them? The capabilities of your phone, even if it is a few years old, are enormous and amazing compared to technology 30 years ago. Taking a minute to think about how amazing this technology is can make you feel a bit more appreciative of the electronics you have, and how they make your life easier.

To create fulfillment in your life, you have to live in the now, and appreciate your life as it is. You can't keep thinking about how great your life will be when you get married, get a promotion, have a bigger apartment, finally live alone, finish writing that book, or lose 10 pounds. Working toward goals is admirable, but you can't sit around waiting to achieve your goals to start loving, appreciating and enjoying your life — that has to start today. And it starts with enjoying what you have in your life at this very moment.

Mindfulness

Like negative visualization, another technique to appreciate what you have is mindfulness. Mindfulness is often confused with meditation in today's society, but the two are extremely similar. Mindfulness is usually seen as a kind of "living" meditation, meaning you can practice it anywhere. You can practice it at your desk at work, while going for a walk, while doing the dishes, or reading a book. You can practice mindfulness anytime, anywhere, and no one needs to know you are doing it.

To practice mindfulness, focus on your five senses: Touch, Smell, Sight, Sound and Taste. Ask yourself what each of these senses is experiencing. What does the keyboard feel like under your fingers at work? Can you hear dogs barking, birds chirping or the wind through the leaves on your walk? Can you see the words on the page as you read a book? What does the dish soap smell like? Even if you are not eating, ask yourself if you can taste anything in your mouth. If not, that's perfectly OK. Even if the answer is "nothing," you are still practicing being aware of your senses.

If you are experienced in practicing mindfulness, you can also observe the rhythm of your breath, your thoughts, and the way your physical body feels during this exercise.

When you practice mindfulness, you have to be in the present moment as you ask yourself these questions. You are concentrating on the here and now. Being more present in the moment has been shown to make people happier. Even if your present situation is not ideal, being present in it is allowing it to just be. When you practice mindfulness, you become more aware of your surroundings, and more in tune with what you have and experience now, instead of living in your thoughts of the past or future. In this way, you will come to appreciate more of what you already have.

Gratitude

The last technique we will use for wanting what we already have is gratitude. Studies show that writing down things we are thankful for just once a day has a huge improvement on our mood and happiness overall. To practice gratitude, you can write a list of three things you are grateful for when you wake up in the morning, or before you got to bed at night. You can choose three separate things, or just one thing and write three reasons you are grateful for it. At first, it may be hard to think of things you are grateful for. But once you start to practice this, you will find that you can be grateful for nearly anything and everything. For example, you may start with a list like this:

I am grateful for my loving spouse

I am grateful to have a job

I am grateful for my health

And eventually end up thinking up creative things to be grateful for, like this:

I am grateful for my feet, and that I can walk from place to place

I am grateful for the stars, and that I get to look at them at night

I am grateful for salt, because it enhances the taste of my meals

It doesn't matter what you write down, as long as you spend a few minutes appreciating what you have to be grateful for in life.

To summarize, the three ways to want what you already have are to practice negative visualization, mindfulness and gratitude. In the first place, though, you have to investigate what feelings are causing you to keep buying, and address those. In the next chapter, we will look at how being frugal — spending less and buying less — can actually be more fun than buying.

FRUGALITY CAN BE FUN

Remember the thought experiment from the first chapter of this book, in which I asked you if you had ever packed for a vacation? To illustrate a little bit of fun frugality to start off this chapter, let's revisit that question.

So, imagine you packed for your beach vacation, and now you've arrived at your destination. But let's say you forgot to bring those essentials: your swimsuit, suntan lotion, and a good book. If you're going to a vacation destination, chances are you could easily buy all three. There are probably shops at the airport you land in that have all three, in fact. You might pay a bit more, but your trip hasn't been ruined. Or, you could probably find a department store that has all three in the city you are visiting. If you are on a remote island, you can still find small shops or your hotel gift shop that will have (if even a small selection) swim suits and sunscreen. Can't find a bookstore? You can download the Kindle app on your phone and buy electronically, borrow a book from another guest or someone you meet on your holiday, or decide to spend vacation writing instead of reading.

In our example, forgetting these essential items was probably a bit of an annoyance, but you figured out how to acquire them. It just took some patience, some creativity, and a bit of luck. Perhaps when you borrowed a book from a fellow traveler, you met someone new and made a lasting connection. Perhaps your garish gift shop swimsuit caused the taxi driver to remember you, and he gives you a discount on your rides the rest of the trip. Perhaps when you forgot your 15 SPF suntan lotion, you had to buy 50 SPF at the store instead. But the sun's heat was intense, and you would had been severely burned and ruined your trip without the higher SPF.

Things will always go wrong in some way. When you are able to ride these mishaps out, you may find that the surprises they have in store are not always bad. Uncertainty is undesirable for humans, as it makes us feel unsafe and uncomfortable, so we try to plan everything out perfectly. That's one reason that we love to acquire things: It feels like it brings a bit of certainty into our lives. But often, it's the things we can't plan for that turn out to be the best part of our experiences.

Now, this is just one example. And buying a second swimsuit may not be frugal, but it is being resourceful. See how resourceful you can be if there's something you don't have, and how easy it can be to acquire it?

One reason that people don't want to get rid of the things they own is that they worry that they will someday need it, and that day will come, and they won't have it. But with Amazon, Wal-Mart and other huge department stores, you can always get anything you really need, if you really need it. And often, you will find that you don't really need something, but there is a way around it, like borrowing it from a neighbor or friend. (Which is even more money-saving!)

When you pare down, you have to accept that you will sometimes have that feeling of "I wish I hadn't gotten rid of that!" But know that it will be OK. Just like in the vacation example, you will bounce back, find a way, and maybe have more fun being creative. It can be easier and more fun to be resourceful than digging through drawers of things to find that one item. And what's the point of carrying one item from house to house every time you move and finding a place to store it just to use it twice in 20 years?

In the next chapter, we will look at another mindset that may help you get rid of your things.

RENTER'S MINDSET

The Renter's Mindset is a way to approach all the things that you feel like you "own" in your life. Do you really "own" them? What does "ownership" mean?

"Ownership," in common terms, means that you have exchanged money with a vendor to acquire the item, you got a receipt of the transaction (a legal document proving that you purchased the item), and you keep it in your home or apartment, with all of the other things you own.

But owning something doesn't take away the certainty of it never leaving you. Maybe you will lose an item walking down the street when it falls out of your bag. Maybe a (God-forbid) house fire takes all of your things away from you by destroying them. "Owning" something does not mean that it brings certainty into your life, or that you can truly own it. Unlike the ancient Egyptians, who believed that you need to bring many possessions with you in your coffin to the after-life, in modern society and many interpretations of the world's great religions, we do not believe that we need to take possessions with us in death, or into an afterlife, which-ever you believe.

Not to get too heavy in this book by bringing up death, but I believe it is important to think about your own death when you think about why you are acquiring things. It may be scary, but it is ultimately freeing, and I believe it makes us live more fully in the present moment. In Ancient Rome, great war heroes would have a slave follow them around to whisper "Momento mori." This Latin phrase roughly translates to "Remember that you will die." It was intended to keep the heroes humble after great victory, but we can co-opt this strategy (without slaves) to keep us mindful of our true values in life.

Like we discussed in the chapter about a life of abundance, it is often intangibles, like our relationships, our work and our health, that bring us true and lasting happiness. Someday, you will die. We all will die. And you cannot bring the latest iPhone with you. You cannot bring your favorite DVD from your collection. You cannot bring your fine China dishes you spent days agonizing over when selecting them for your wedding registry. So why worry so much about these things?

Some people might argue that this sort of thinking leads to nihilism, or the belief that nothing matters and life is meaningless. But I see two choices you can make. One, yes, is nihilism. But the other is adopting the Renter's Mindset in life.

So what is the Renter's Mindset? The Renter's Mindset is the opposite of the owner's mindset. The renter recognizes that "ownership" is a false feeling of certainty, and that we are truly renting ever single thing in our lives, including our possessions, our home (even if we "own" it), our relationships, and especially, our time on this Earth. Once you wrap your head around this more philosophical concept, you will be able to approach things with less anxiety and more freedom. You will not need to worry about buying the latest gadget or get wrapped up in "keeping up with the Joneses." You will not feel the superficial pull of these things when you are able to see yourself as just borrowing each of the items you buy. You will not feel afraid of losing the things you acquire (or feel so much pressure to acquire them) when you realize you will have to give them up eventually, no matter what.

The Renter's Mindset is a bit ethereal and philosophical, so do not worry if you don't really get it or don't find it helps you in your minimalism quest. Take and apply what you find helpful from these philosophical chapters, and feel free to discard what you don't. (In true minimalist fashion!)

This chapter concludes our more philosophical discussions of minimalism, and in the rest of the book, we will get to practical applications of minimalism, and how declutter your home, your digital life and your schedule.

DECLUTTERING PRINCIPLES

As we prepare for the decluttering chapters of this book, let's look at a few general principles that we can apply as we go through our things. These general principles will guide you as you make decisions of what to keep and what to get rid of.

If you can decide on some general rules, values and principles before starting decluttering, you will have a handy list of heuristics (rules of thumb) to reference when you are having trouble making a decision.

Here are few decluttering principles you may find helpful when you get stuck:

1. If you haven't used an item in the last 12 months, and you could easily acquire it again for under $20, you should get rid of it. (It will be difficult to put this into practice. Getting rid of something when you think you should keep it "just in case," is hard, but with each thing you release, it will become easier. Remember to have the Renter's Mindset)

2. Did you remember you had this item? If you didn't know you had it, you probably haven't been missing it. This item can be let go of.

3. Have you used this item in the last six months? Outside of season-specific clothes, if you haven't used something in the last six months, you rarely use it, and keeping it around is probably causing more of a drain on your resources (atorage, care, loss of resale value) than it is worth. You can play with this number to see how it suits you. Maybe you want to do three months. Or one year. Choose what feels best and what helps you make the best decluttering decisions for you.

Those three guiding principles will help you get rid of most of the objects that are cluttering your life needlessly. De-cluttering and minimizing is a process that, if done right, will take a bit of time. While it is not good to sit and agonize over decisions forever, if you declutter too quickly, you will not have gone through the process in an emotional way, and you will probably find yourself filling up your home again with needless items. You have to stay mindful of the big picture, and not each specific item.

So, as you delve into these next four decluttering chapters, keep in mind *why* you are decluttering. That is why the philosophical chapters of this book are so important. Once you start going through your items, the task may feel daunting, impossible, emotionally exhausting, and not worth it.

If you can, write down a short list of what you can gain by decluttering.

For example:

If I declutter the spare bedroom, I can have more friends and family visit, and strengthening those relationships will bring me happiness.

If I declutter the kitchen, I will have more room to cook healthy meals that make me feel good.

If I get rid of half of my wardrobe, I won't have to spend

as much time deciding what to wear in the morning, and I can get more sleep.

This list will remind you just why you are taking on this difficult task, and keep you motivated.

Now, onto the decluttering!

DECLUTTER YOUR HOME

Decluttering your home may be the hardest decluttering task you face, depending on how large your home is and how many things you have acquired over the years. Even if you live in a simple studio apartment, it is worth going through your things.

Your initial declutter will probably take a while, but once you have completed it, you will only need minimal maintenance forever after. Once you are aware of why you are brining so many items into your life, you will stop wanting them and buying them. You may even find you will keep getting rid of more and more things over the years, as you fill your life up with abundance in other ways.

For the first round of decluttering, you don't need to accomplish this all in a weekend, and I advise you don't. You will feel rushed, stressed, emotionally overwhelmed, and probably have a breakdown and want to give up. I suggest focusing on one room each weekend, and taking a month or two to go through all your things. It's not a race to minimalism, remember. Proceed at your own pace, and with what feels right.

If you don't live alone, it should be noted that you will need to bring up the topic of your newfound minimalism with the people you live with. You can't get rid of something someone else owns, or something someone else felt was a commonly-owned item shared by everyone in your living space. How you want to approach this conversation varies, but shouldn't be taken lightly. If you are serious about committing to a fuller, richer and simpler life, you will need to convey your seriousness to your roommates, children, spouse, or whomever you live with. They may judge you or think you are crazy for wanting to get rid of all the wonderful stuff you own. Prepare for this reaction, but know that you are making the right decision for your life. Let them know that you will be going through your own items, but will not disrupt their things. You can explain why you are making the change, and you may find that they become a bit interested in minimalism.

However, many people are not so interested in living a life of minimalism. They may say, "I wish I could do that, but I just need all my things" or "I wish I could do what you do, but I just love shopping too much." People love to make excuses about why they can't change, and you can't force anyone to change. However, you can make steps to make sure they don't prevent you from changing. When I first started practicing minimalism, I knew I'd take a lot of my things to the Goodwill to donate them. I wanted someone else to be able to use the things that I didn't. So, I thought it was kind to offer my friends and family members first-pick to use the items I knew I would be happier without. But this caused me more grief than pleasure. People would not only keep nearly everything I tried to give away, they'd judge me in the process. "Woah, you're just throwing this away?" they'd ask. "How could you get rid of this? I'll keep it for you until you want it back." So beware of letting your friends and family be too involved in the process if they do not have the same mindset as you.

As you go through the rooms of your home, there is a process that I recommend for decluttering. The process can take a bit of time, so make sure you have a few days to really commit to it, otherwise you (or your housemates) may go crazy from all the stuff you've pulled out and left everywhere.

First, you should pull everything in a room out. Yes, everything. Drawers, cabinets, closets, find it all. Then, start going through everything, item by item. You will have three piles into which to put things: Yes/Keep, No/Get Rid Of and Maybe.

Yes/Keep items are things that you immediately know you use. You have used it in the last week for sure, and maybe you use it almost every day. It's something that you find incredibly helpful, and is an item that fits the 20% part of the 80/20 Rule (You get 80% of the use out of 20% of your things.)

No/Get Rid Of items are things you can't remember using, or haven't used in the last six months to a year. They fall in the 80% of the 80/20 rule. (80% of your things you use 20% of the time). Here is where it is easy to fall into the "what-if" and the "just-in-case" trap. You imagine in your head a scenario where you will need the thing in an emergency, if some unusual situation comes up, or if you finally host that dinner party you've talked about hosting but never have for the last 10 years. Well, dear reader and newfound minimalist, it is time: Time to finally let go. Time to finally accept your life. Time to be more free. If you can replace the item fairly easily (at a store within a short drive, or a purchase on Amazon) for less than $20, it should go.

The Maybe items will be the trickiest. They will be the things that you find sentimental value in, that you use sometimes but not very often, or that you're just not sure about. That is OK. Don't let a Maybe item stall you for hours as you contemplate its usefulness. Just recognize a Maybe item when you see it and put it in the Maybe pile. Maybe items will be put in storage, out of sight, so they can not easily be gotten, for three months or six months. If you haven't missed an item, or found it worth it to go digging through packed-away boxes to pull it out, then you can safely get rid of it after the allotted time you have chosen. You won't even need to open the Maybe boxes and go through all the items again, as it will cause you further grief and anguish trying to decide once again if the Maybe items are worth keeping or not. When the three months, or six months, or however long you decide on, is up, just grab the boxes, don't look inside, and drop them off at the Goodwill. Decisions made!

Of course, there will be some exceptions to these rules, and I'll discuss a few special cases and considerations below:

Bedroom

Making your bedroom as comfortable and simple as possible may help you sleep at night. Many people use their bedrooms as a place to work, get distracted by their phone and scroll endlessly for a long time, pay bills, or do a lot of things besides intentional relaxing and sleep. If you make your bedroom a place solely for sleep and pre-sleep relaxation, like reading or your end-of-day gratitude lists, your brain will instantly shift into "sleep mode" when you are in your bedroom. I recommend that you think about making your bedroom a place of rest when you declutter, as sleep is such an important part of a healthy life.

Books

If you are an avid reader (as you probably are if you've picked up this little book), you may have an extensive collection of books that you are proud of. I once owned hundreds of books. The problem was, most of them were unread. They were "someday" books. They were aspirational books. They were the books I'd probably have time to read when I also got that promotion, lost 10 pounds, and had a chic wardrobe. My bookshelf also involved many of my favorites, book that I actually *had* read. But I wasn't pulling them out to read them every day. In fact, I wasn't re-reading them even once a year. That meant my book collection, while it looked nice, wasn't doing a whole lot for my day-to-day-life. It was part of the 80% of my possessions I was using 20% of the time (Or realistically, maybe 1%). I spent a ton of money on books, as I loved browsing bookstores and reading "Best Books" lists, but I never seemed to get around to actually reading them or finishing them.

Now, I've embraced libraries and digital books. While you may have to wait a bit longer to borrow a library book, rather than buying it at a bookstore, it is good exercise in patience, and has significantly cut down my impulse purchases. I now use a Kindle reader to read many books as well, which has cut down my bookshelf space quite a bit. I got rid of all my books, and know that with the internet, anything I need to reference can be found with only a few clicks. Getting rid of books doesn't mean you aren't a reader or a bookworm, if that is a large part of your identity. It just means that you don't need a bookshelf full of books to portray yourself that way to people, and you can still read as much as your heart desires through other means.

Collectibles

Many people are avid collectors. Maybe you collect postcards of your travels, model trains, DVDs of your favorite movies, or rare editions of books. If your collection is very important to you, and it brings joy into your life, then of course, don't get rid of it. Minimalism is about deciding what is important to you, and cutting out what isn't important, and what is just a clutter and distraction. So if you really get joy out of your collection, keep it. However, really think about your collection before automatically deciding to keep it. Another essential aspect of minimalism is investigating the emotional reasons for having things. So as long as you spend some time thinking about it, considering your reasons, and decide it is part of your new abundant but simple life, then you are good.

Garage

Growing up, my family garage was rarely used for an actual car. It was most often used to store a ton of toys, lawn equipment, and miscellaneous junk. I advise trying to use your garage for your car. But it may mean getting rid of a lot of items.

Sentimental Items

Items that hold sentimental value are one of the most difficult categories to work through when decluttering your home. It is easy to keep every birthday greeting card we ever receive, every gift we get, and every receipt from a memorable vacation. But are these things bringing abundance and happiness to your life, or are you only keeping them because you fear getting rid of them? One helpful way to think about your sentimental items is to realize that if you keep everything, then it reduces the value of your sentimental items. However, if you only keep the most sentimental, then you have made those few items very important. If you have 300 school assignments from your grade school days, or those of your children, it can feel very emotional and cruel to get rid of them. But how often do you sit down and go through all 300 of these? If you go through the stack and pick five or 10 that you find very meaningful, you can keep these. Maybe you can even choose just one, and then you can frame it and hang it up in a place of prominence in your home. Then, instead of having 300 pages and projects gathering dust and never appreciated, you have just one item that you can look at and appreciate every day. It doesn't mean you don't care, it just means that you are caring intentionally and in a way that makes sense.

It is the same with greeting cards or gifts. If you have kept every card your aunt has ever sent you, they, too, are probably in a box hiding somewhere. You know what would be more meaningful than keeping all her cards, something neither you, nor her, probably think about on a daily basis, or ever? Call up your aunt and take her to lunch. That hour you spend talking with her is much more aligned with living an abundant life than keeping her cards. The next logical step to consider, however, is the death of a loved one. If your aunt has passed, getting rid of her cards may seem cruel. In this case, I'd recommend the grade school art strategy. Choose something that would make you think of your aunt and how much she meant to you, and display it somewhere. This is more meaningful than keeping an object just because. And remember that what is most important in our lives is the people themselves, and our relationships with those people do not exist in objects. They exist in our experiences, memories and feelings. You have the power to remember them, the power does not lie in physical things.

One way to "keep" sentimental items without having to physically store them is to take digital photos of them, or scan them into your computer. You can keep digital photos, which will be nice reminders if you want to pass them down in your family, but then no one is responsible for keeping boxes and boxes of things.

Seasonal Items

Christmas decorations, other holiday decorations or seasonal wear will be harder to assess than everyday items, as you use them occasionally but maybe have not in the last six months. Some of the regular rules apply, though. Remember that less is more. Do you need all the Christmas decorations you have, or could you pare down to just the things you really love and get joy from? We will discuss clothing in a following chapter.

I hope this list has given you the tools you need to get started on decluttering your home. Do you have a conundrum in your decluttering, or a question about this chapter? As you go through your decluttering journey, if you want to reach out to me about something from this book, I am happy to help. You can reach me at contact@walnutpub.com, and put in the subject "To Aston."

In the next chapter, we will look at decluttering your digital life, another important aspect of all of our lives in this day and age.

DECLUTTER YOUR DEVICES

In this chapter, we will discuss decluttering your digital life and devices. In this day and age, we all live so much of our lives online. We shop online, we social network online, we send email instead of letters, we work online, we read on a digital device, we listen to music on our phone or computer, we take digital photos that we may never print out. We do everything online, and sometimes it can feel like our digital existence is as cluttered, if not more so, than our physical one.

While all the information from our online lives is digital, and it therefore doesn't take up a lot of space in our physical life, it still weighs on us mentally. It is still clutter that can make us feel anxious, like our minds are constantly racing, and like we have too much to do and too much going on.

So paring down your digital life is also important to living a life of minimalism, and enjoying a life of abundance.

How can you minimize your digital life?

Pare Down Your Apps & Notifications

Looking at a cluttered phone screen sends our mind

racing. With so many apps to check, and apps that send us notifications, our attention gets diverted and divided thousands of times throughout the day. Keep only the apps that you find truly essential, that you really need, or that you really get good use out of. It can take just 15 minutes to go through and declutter your phone by erasing old apps you downloaded but never use, get rid of distracting and time-wasting games, and hiding your other time-wasting apps on screens other than your home screen. If you have a bad habit of checking your phone and unlocking it often, but after decluttering you can unlock it to a very simple or blank screen, you will be less likely to check it all the time moving forward. Having a decluttered screen can feel like having a decluttered mind.

Organize Your Files

Decluttering can be the same on your laptop, desktop computer or an external hard drive. Organize your documents so that you know where to find them. You may find that you can delete a lot of old documents as well, or move them all into an "old documents" folder. Once you know that all your old files have been sorted, you will feel fresher.

Check Social Media/Email Less Frequently

It is a bad habit to check your phone all the time, and doing this habit on a daily basis actually rewires your brain for scattered, shallow and distracted thinking. You get better at jumping from task to task, but you sacrifice the ability to concentrate, think deeply, or work hard on something for a sustained period. Breaking this habit is essential to reclaiming your mind, and truly 'decluttering' your brain.

Unsubscribe with Abandon

One tactic that can help with feeling like you are always behind on emails, work and catching up on notifications is unsubscribing from as much as you can. Whenever you sign up for a website, buy something online, or sign up for a service, you get subscribed by email to a newsletter of some kind. These newsletters can quickly get out of control. The best way to keep your email inbox clean is to prevent the emails from coming in in the first place. Unsubscribe from as much as you can. Even if you fear missing out on a piece of news, or one deal, is it really worth it to read that one news article or get 10% off a certain item, if instead you can reclaim all that time you waste opening and discarding the hundreds of emails it takes to find the relevant one? I personally have unsubscribed from so many emails that now, the only emails I receive that are not work-related are personal email from friends and family, and one newsletter from a website I like reading that comes once every two weeks. As soon as I am auto-added to a new email list, I immediately unsubscribe. This strategy has helped erase so much digital clutter in my life, and I can rest easy knowing that my inbox is always clean and only contains emails that are actually relevant to me.

Have Intentional Disconnected Time

Most of us spend 100% of our time "connected." We get email notifications on our phones, check our social media sites every hour (if not every 15 minutes), and are available at any time to receive a phone call or text from someone and respond. But this constant connectedness is having a negative impact on our lives. We sometimes ignore the people we love when we spend time with them by checking our phone. Our brains become easily distracted, and we find it difficult to focus. We crave constant information and distraction.

Practicing intentional time to disconnect from it all will feel incredibly uncomfortable at first. Going for a 15-minute walk without your phone might make you feel naked. What if there is an emergency? What if you get lost and need

GPS? What if you get an important email? These irrational fears keep us tethered to our phones. Instead, take a deep breath, and realize that there is nothing so important that it can't wait 15 minutes. Practice going places without your phone, or leaving your phone in another room of the house when you are trying to focus on reading a book or getting a task done. It will take your practice, but over time, you will begin to relish the time you can spend disconnected. You will find you can focus better, you don't constantly crave distraction, and you feel more relaxed.

Overall, doing some digital declutter maintenance will make you feel a bit less scattered. But in addition to organizing our devices and files, it is also a good minimalist habit to not need to feel connected to many social networking sites and email constantly. While these sites can be a good way to share with friends and family and keep in touch, not to mention stay on top of work, they lead to a distracted mind. A decluttered mind is one that can appreciate the here and now, and not get lost in a cycle of instant gratification.

In the next chapter, we will look at decluttering your time and schedule.

DECLUTTER YOUR SCHEDULE

Sometimes, it can feel like there is so much to do. We are busy at work, we are busy in our home lives, we are busy in our free time. It can feel like there is just no time. We want to get to the gym, but there is no time. We want to start a daily writing habit, but there is just no time. We want to spend more time with someone we care about, but we just can't find the time.

Being a minimalist with your time means going back to that tenet of minimalism: Cut out the inessential, to allow the essential to grow abundantly.

What Brings You Satisfaction?

Here, the 80/20 rule comes into play again. What tasks are you spending 80% of your time on, but only getting 20% of the results in your life from? For example, are you doing an easy workout for 90 minutes, when you could be doing a very difficult workout in 30 minutes? Are you splitting your attention between social media, email, and your work tasks? Studies show that multitasking actually leads to completing fewer tasks in a timely manner. You could instead focus on one thing at a time and see much better results. Are there activities you could just eliminate from your life entirely to cut down on wasted time?

For example, what you doing because you feel like you "need" to, or are "supposed to," but you don't actually want to? Do you feel like you should be gardening to keep up with the neighbors, but you don't actually get that much satisfaction from it, and would rather spend your time doing yoga, or re-connecting with friends, or writing, or anything else? You could either hire a gardener, or just let the lawn go natural. You get to decide what is worth your limited time on this Earth to do, and should not feel trapped in what other people think is important.

Keep Track

One tactic to use when you are trying to declutter your schedule is to keep track of what you spend your time on. When people are trying to stick to a diet, they are often told to keep a food diary. It is the same for budgeting and spending. When you have to write down what you eat or spend, you become more aware of it, and have data to see what is really going on.

So keep a log of your time for a week or a month, and it will definitely surprise you. Log every minute, if you can. How long does your morning routine take? How much time do you spend online? How much time watching TV? How much time at the gym? Log everything, and then see where you are "overspending" your time, and what essential activities that you claim are important to you are actually getting the short end of the stick.

Say No

It can be difficult to say "no" to someone. Many of us like to please other people. We like to be helpful, agreeable and nice. Saying "no" without a concrete excuse can feel like being rude and selfish. But learning how to say "no" is freeing. We all have obligations that we feel like we can't change. We have to be in the office for a certain number of hours per week, we have to help that junior coworker who asked for mentorship, we have to attend our friend's barbecue, we have to go the gym seven days a week to maintain our fitness.

With your new minimalist mindset, however, you should question whether these non-negotiables are really that non-negotiable. If you are trying to declutter your time and schedule, look once again at what is bringing you the most satisfaction and happiness, and what you are attending out of feelings of obligation.

Let's look at some examples. For the junior coworker who wants mentorship, you would feel guilty if you said no. But is it really best for her to have a mentor who feels like they have to say yes, versus a mentor who is actually very excited to take her under their wing? For your friend's barbecue, do you feel like you have to attend because you have nothing else going on that day, but you actually aren't excited about it? Do you imagine all the things you could get done if you had that Saturday afternoon free? People often feel like they have to have a reason to say no to something. But you may be surprised how much people respect a firm "no" given without an excuse. If you just say, "I'm sorry, but I won't be able to attend," most polite people won't probe further to ask you why. They will respect your "no." We often feel in our society that spending time just by ourselves is not a valid excuse to say no. But why shouldn't your priorities and values be the best reason to say no? If you have dedicated Saturday afternoons as the time you take up the guitar and practice, then just because you have scheduled that time by yourself, and are only accountable to yourself, that doesn't mean it's not a great reason to turn down social invitations. Don't be afraid of saying a simple "no." Stand up for yourself and your time. It's the only way to make sure there's enough time in the day for the things that are important to you. Saying "yes" to every opportunity, invitation and request that comes your way is a sure-fire way to stay over-scheduled, stretched thin and stressed.

Now let's look at the other two obligations: Your job and your fitness. For your job, you may be surprised just how negotiable your job is. You feel you have to be at work 40 hours per week, but what if you asked your boss for a work-from-home day once every two weeks? With remote work becoming more and more mainstream, this request may not be as unreasonable as you think. Saving one day of commute, being able to throw a load of laundry in during the day, and being able to be home for a repair or service worker to come by the home will save hours of time in your week. You may have to start small, and prove to your boss you are actually working just as hard at home by doing a few trial afternoons, but don't think that working from home is too extreme of an idea.

Minimalism is about questioning the status-quo, when it comes to our objects and our time. Women are stereotypically supposed to have at least a dozen pairs of shoes, but why? You have to investigate these beliefs that you may not have questioned before, just like the belief that it is necessary for you to be in your office to get work done.

As for fitness, maintaining a healthy lifestyle is important. But when it comes to trimming your obligations and freeing up more time, ask yourself, "Am I working harder, or smarter?" Getting to the gym seven days a week is admirable, but could you be cutting out one or two workouts a week, and letting your muscles relax with rest days? Could you change your workout style to do more impactful exercises just three or four days a week? Can you listen to an audiobook during your workout, and therefore read and exercise at the same time? Try to question the things you see as set in stone, and you may find that you can free up so much more time in your day that you thought possible.

In minimalism, managing your time and energy is as important as managing your stuff. In the next chapter, we will look at decluttering your closet.

CAPSULE WARDROBE

The 80/20 rule especially applies to our wardrobe. You have your favorite outfits, shirts, accessories and items. Imagine these items in your mind. When you wear them, you probably feel the most "you." They fit your personality, and your style. They make you feel good about your body and the way you look. You probably wear these clothes 80% of the time. Most of your clothes just sit in your closet, and you only wear them occasionally. Maybe they don't fit quite right, or the color, in retrospect, doesn't look that great on you. Maybe you can't quite place your finger on why you don't enjoy wearing that clothing, but for some reason, it sits unworn in your closet most of the time. It is part of the 80% of your clothes that you wear 20% of the time.

The capsule wardrobe is the idea of a style of dress that comes from French origins. The idea is to have classic and basic clothing items that you love, and that can all be mixed and matched with each other. With just a total of 30 items, you create dozens if not hundreds of different looks, once you add in different shoes and accessories.

Now, the capsule wardrobe might not be for you. Maybe you love bright colors or flashy patterns, and having just a few items that all go together wouldn't work with your personal style. That's OK, the idea of a capsule wardrobe is to realize the things that you wear most, and treat those items with care.

Another thing to think about when it comes to clothes is investing in quality. "Fast fashion" stores like H&M and Forever 21 produce extremely cheap clothes that are highly fashionable. But they tend to wear down very quickly, and you have to keep buying new clothes. However, if you purchase high-quality, classic clothing items, you can keep these clothing items around for years if you take care of them.

Most people won't notice if you simplify your wardrobe. People are too self-focused to notice that you have a minimal, classic style that you recycle often. In fact, you will look very well put-together all the time. Wouldn't it be great to feel stylish, the most "you," and comfortable all of the time, instead of feeling like you need to wear your clothes you don't really like sometimes, just because they're there?

Simplifying your wardrobe means that you will have fewer decisions to make in the course of the day, especially when you first wake up and need your brain power to focus on more important tasks. You will find that you save so much time and stress over what to wear, and instead, you will be able to divert that time and attention on to more meaningful parts of your life, just like when you pare down your possessions, your schedule, and your devices.

I recommend decluttering your closet in the same fashion as you decluttered the rest of your house. Those tips can be found in the "Declutter Your Home" chapter. Go once again through making Keep, Discard and Maybe piles, and keep the Maybe items hidden for a certain amount of time. Following those steps, you can free up your closet space and trim your wardrobe.

In the next and final chapter, we will discuss a closing though on minimalism and essentialism.

CONCLUSION: ESSENTIALISM

Thank you for reading this guide to minimalism. We covered a lot of ground about this philosophy of life, including emotional questioning, practical tips for decluttering, and what it all means and what it's all for. What I hope you take away from this book is that minimalism doesn't need to mean getting rid of as much stuff as you can. It is all about essentialism. Get rid of what is inessential to become abundant in what is essential.

Minimalism is tailor-made for me, for you, and for everyone. Choose how much of it you want to adopt in your life. If you want to have a huge wardrobe, and you genuinely get joy out of wearing each piece of clothing you have, then own as many clothes as you like. If you love your Trolls collection with all your heart, then keep them. Don't let anyone else judge your possessions or tell you what should matter to you.

However, that doesn't mean minimalism is simple. Making the distinction between the essential and the inessential can be difficult. The lines are often gray, not black and white, and it's hard to figure out what feels good right now versus what feels good in a healthy, real and sustaining way over a lifetime. Choosing a life of minimalism means really investigating what you have that makes you happy, and what is extra, wasteful and a drag on your time, resources and energy. Cut out all that extra stuff without mercy and focus on only what will truly matter, in the end, to you.

Our time on this Earth is limited. Our brain chemistry seeks out what is instant, flashy and seductive. Often, that means shopping and purchasing and hoarding things we don't need. It means apps that notify us and ping us for interaction as often as possible for little tangible reward. It means overbooked schedules so that we never have to miss out, say "no," or really invest deeply. But minimalism is here to liberate you from all that noise. You don't need all that. You're better than that. I'm better than that. And we all deserve better than that.

I hope that your journey with minimalism has begun here, but that it leads to a lifelong journey of noticing your life, living with intentionality, experiencing life more deeply, and choosing what you spend your time and money on, instead of letting your impulses choose for you. I sincerely believe you can choose to be happier with a life of minimalism.

I sincerely hope that you begin to lead a life of abundance once you adopt some or all of the principles of minimalism. It may not be easy at first, but it is worth all the hard work you will put in, I can guarantee that.

Thanks for reading.

DID YOU ENJOY THIS BOOK?

I personally read every review my books receive.

I look forward to reading yours.

Please leave a review on Amazon by visiting your recent orders page or searching for the title of this book.

With Gratitude,
Aston Sanderson

ABOUT THE AUTHOR: ASTON SANDERSON

Aston Sanderson is passionate about helping people lead better lives through short, conversational and fun books. He is the author of "Small Talk," a manual for better conversations, "Self Talk," a guide to practicing more self-love, and "Minimalist Living," a helpful way to declutter your life. He loves to hear from readers at aston@walnutpub.com for book feedback and ideas of what readers want to learn about next. His books are available in many languages worldwide.

24038506R00142

Printed in Great Britain
by Amazon